LEVEL D

CONTENTS

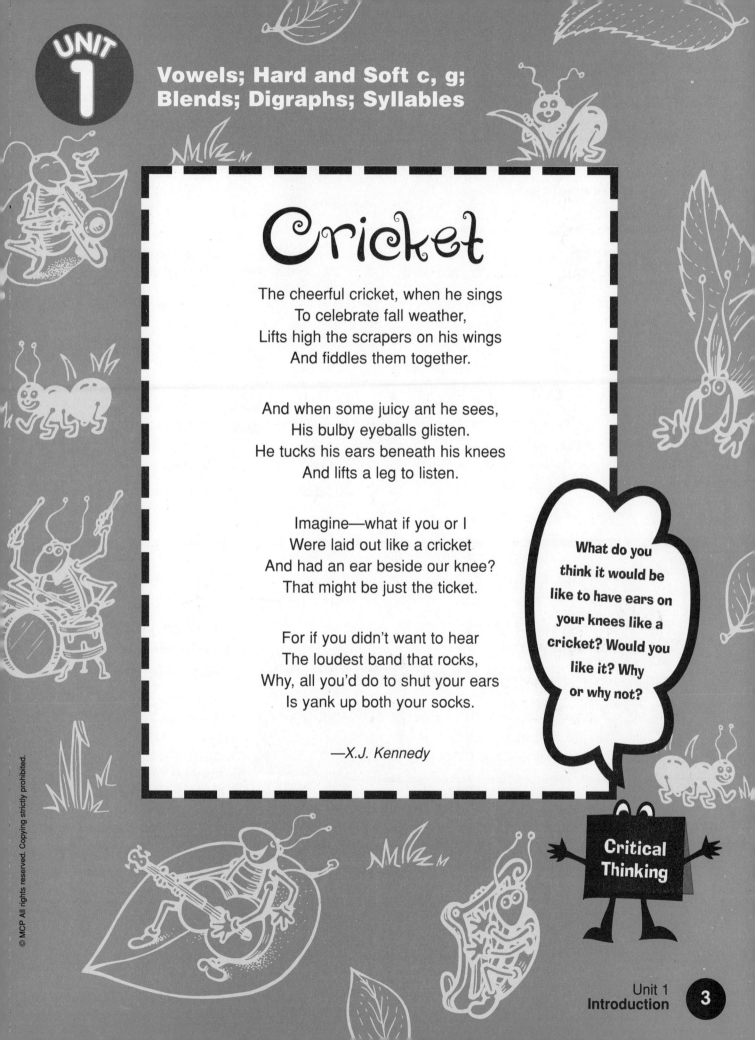

Cricket

The cheerful cricket, when he sings
To celebrate fall weather,
Lifts high the scrapers on his wings
And fiddles them together.

And when some juicy ant he sees,
His bulby eyeballs glisten.
He tucks his ears beneath his knees
And lifts a leg to listen.

Imagine—what if you or I
Were laid out like a cricket
And had an ear beside our knee?
That might be just the ticket.

For if you didn't want to hear
The loudest band that rocks,
Why, all you'd do to shut your ears
Is yank up both your socks.

—X.J. Kennedy

What do you think it would be like to have ears on your knees like a cricket? Would you like it? Why or why not?

Critical Thinking

Dear Family,

During the next few weeks, your child will be learning about words with long and short vowel sounds, the hard and soft sounds of c and g, blends, and consonant digraphs.

At-Home Activities

▶ Read the poem "Cricket" on the other side of this letter with your child. Together, look for words with the hard and soft sounds of c (cricket, celebrate) and g (leg, imagine); blends with r (cricket), l (glisten), and s (scrapers); final blends (ant, band); and the consonant digraphs sh (shut), th (them), and wh (when).

▶ Look through newspapers and magazines to find words with the sounds and spellings we will be studying in this unit.

▶ Visit your local library or use magazine articles to learn more about crickets. Have your child write five interesting facts about crickets.

Book Corner

You and your child might enjoy reading these books together.

Beetles, Lightly Toasted

by Phyllis Reynolds Naylor

Andy enters an essay contest proposing the idea of eating insects. When he wins he has to sample his own recipes.

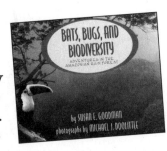

Bats, Bugs, and Biodiversity

by Susan Goodman

A trip through the Amazon rainforests with a group of students teaches about the balance of the ecosystem.

Sincerely,

_____

Name _____

Circle the word in each pair in which you hear a final blend.

1. tin — tint
2. king — kit
3. cat — cast
4. think — thin
5. hunt — hut
6. ramp — ram
7. ten — tend
8. wink — win
9. risk — rise
10. wan — want
11. cramp — cram
12. chump — chum
13. base — bask
14. bun — bunt
15. mat — mast
16. pain — paint
17. on — bond
18. bend — Ben
19. toad — toast
20. bad — band

Read each definition. Then write the word from the word bank that goes with it. Circle the blends in the words you write.

mask	plank	print	sink	stump
rent	limp	coast	vest	blend

21. a basin in the kitchen that has a drain and water faucets _____

22. a kind of jacket without sleeves _____

23. the part of the tree left after it has been cut down _____

24. the edge of land facing the sea _____

25. to walk in a lame way _____

26. to mix together _____

27. the kind of mark often made by a foot or finger _____

28. a face covering with openings for the eyes _____

29. a long, wide, thick board _____

30. money paid for the use of an apartment _____

1. Each _____ of animal has its own way of moving.　　　　　　　　　mind　　kind

2. Animals run, crawl, hop, and _____ .　　　　　　　　　thump　　jump

3. Some animals _____ their days in treetops.　　　　　　　　　spend　　stamp

4. They have strong arms and hands to _____ branches.　　　　　　　　　grasp　　wasp

5. They _____ be able to hold on tightly.　　　　　　　　　rest　　must

6. Other animals live on the _____ .　　　　　　　　　ground　　plank

7. Some _____ other animals for food.　　　　　　　　　point　　hunt

8. Others are at _____ of being eaten.　　　　　　　　　mask　　risk

9. Both kinds must be able to move _____ .　　　　　　　　　fast　　vest

10. Most have strong front and _____ legs.　　　　　　　　　band　　hind

11. People and apes have both feet and _____ .　　　　　　　　　sands　　hands

12. Apes like _____ live in trees and on the ground.　　　　　　　　　chimps　　lamps

13. Chimps' spines _____ at an angle.　　　　　　　　　bend　　send

14. On the ground, chimps walk _____ over.　　　　　　　　　tent　　bent

15. They walk on their feet and their _____ knuckles.　　　　　　　　　front　　want

16. People's straight spines help them _____ upright.　　　　　　　　　stand　　tend

17. This leaves our hands free for any _____ .　　　　　　　　　whisk　　task

18. Don't you _____ this is a good way to be?　　　　　　　　　thank　　think

Critical Thinking

Why are apes able to climb in trees and walk on the ground?

Name

Magic: Tricks and Treats!

Magic has given pleasure to people all over the world for thousands of years. Records from ancient Egypt describe magicians who made small statues appear to turn into live crocodiles. In India, magicians of the past developed a trick that is still famous today. A young boy climbs up a long rope thrown into the air and seems to disappear at the top.

One of the most spectacular stunts in modern magic is sawing a woman in half. This trick was invented in 1920 by a British magician, P. T. Selbit. His assistant was placed in a wooden box from which only her head protruded. All she had to do was draw her knees up under her chin while he sawed. An American magician, Harry Goldin, improved the trick in 1921. His assistant's head, hands, and feet could be seen clearly as he sawed her in half. What do you think was the secret of this trick? (Turn page upside down.)

Magicians of the present try to improve on tricks created by magicians of the past as well as invent their own illusions. To interest audiences, magicians wear special clothes, wave magic wands, and speak magic words. We do not think that what we are seeing is real. We know we are being fooled, but somehow we still believe it!

Answer: There were two women in the box.

Why do people enjoy seeing magicians perform, even though they know they are being fooled?

_____

_____

_____

_____

_____

Lesson 8

Review short and long vowels; hard and soft c, g; blends: Reading

Writing

Write a description of your favorite magic trick and tell how you think it was done. Draw a diagram in the space below to show how the trick works. Use some of the words from the word bank. The questions below may help you.

Helpful Hints

Who did the trick?

Where did you see it?

What happened?

Why is this your favorite trick?

How do you think it is done?

split	true
bend	special
center	change
hands	flap
went	risk

Review short and long vowels; hard and soft c, g; blends: Writing

Digraph	Beginning	Middle	Ending
sh	**sh**ip	a**sh**es	fi**sh**
th	**th**ing	mo**th**er	tee**th**
ch	**ch**icks	ex**ch**ange	wat**ch**
wh	**wh**en	a**wh**ile	—

> **Circle two pictures in each row whose names contain the consonant digraph sound you hear in the first word. Write the words on the lines.**

DEFINITION

A **consonant digraph** is two or more consonants that together represent one sound.

1 brush

_____ _____ _____

2 thirty

_____ _____ _____

3 wheat

_____ _____ _____

> **Read each sentence. Circle the word that correctly completes the sentence and write it on the line.**

4. Mr. Batt is the _____ of the football team. cough coach

5. He wears a shiny _____ around his neck. thistle whistle

6. The players _____ equipment onto the field. wheel wreath

7. Mr. Batt warns them about a _____ of mud. patch peach

8. The players wear large _____ pads. shudder shoulder

9. Some players will _____ the ball. throw chow

10. Other players will _____ the ball and run. catch rich

Computers: Machines That Think

In 1822, Charles Babbage asked the British government for funds to build what he called a Difference Engine. He said that this machine could add, subtract, multiply, and divide. Babbage got some money, but the machine was never finished.

Babbage also had thought up a machine—called an Analytical Engine—that could do more complex math. The government refused to give him money for this machine, because they said, "There is no possible use for it." The British government did not know that one day computers would do much more than solve math problems. Today, computers control other machines, guide ships, launch the space shuttle, and play chess. Most important, they can be programmed to think.

Before the microprocessor was introduced in 1971, computers were huge and slow. Their switches were thousands of bulky valves that looked something like lightbulbs. Memories, which were stored on magnetic drums, could fill whole rooms.

The microprocessor, contained in a single chip, changed the computer industry. Though it is as small as a shirt button, the modern microchip can store enormous amounts of information. It is these tiny chips that make laptop computers possible.

How are today's computers different from Charles Babbage's Difference Engine?

Critical Thinking

1. What would Babbage's Difference Engine have done?

_____

2. What kinds of things do modern computers do?

_____

_____

_____

3. How big were the early computers?

_____

4. What invention made laptop computers possible?

_____

5. How is the size of a microchip described?

_____

Read the sentences and underline each word that contains **ch**. Write the word you underlined under **church** if **ch** stands for its usual sound. Write the word under **chef** if **ch** has the **sh** sound, or under **chord** if **ch** stands for the **k** sound.

RULE

Usually **ch** stands for the sound you hear at the beginning and end of **church**. Sometimes **ch** can stand for the **sh** sound or the **k** sound.

chipmunk   **ch**ef   **ch**emist

1. Mr. Christy took our school choir and orchestra on a field trip.

2. He chauffeured us to a restaurant called the Chic Steakhouse.

3. Pictures of cartoon characters were on the walls.

4. A large, bright chandelier hung from the ceiling.

5. Every table had a vase of fresh chrysanthemums.

6. The chef, Charlene, made delicious chicken.

7. Our waitress, Charlotte, served us with a smile.

8. The chocolate chiffon pie was their specialty.

9. I had grapes and cherries for dessert.

10. At the end of the meal, our teacher paid the check.

11. He left the extra change for our waitress.

12. We, as a chorus, cheered her.

(**church**)   (**chef**)   (**chord**)

_____   _____   _____

_____   _____   _____

_____   _____   _____

_____   _____   _____

_____   _____   _____

_____   _____   _____

Read each word below and circle its consonant digraph. Then write the word in the correct column according to whether the consonant digraph comes at the beginning, in the middle, or at the end of the word.

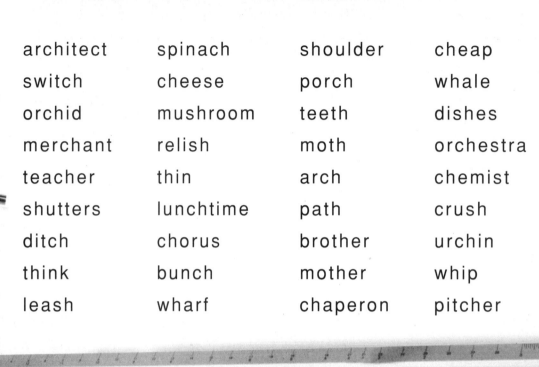

architect	spinach	shoulder	cheap
switch	cheese	porch	whale
orchid	mushroom	teeth	dishes
merchant	relish	moth	orchestra
teacher	thin	arch	chemist
shutters	lunchtime	path	crush
ditch	chorus	brother	urchin
think	bunch	mother	whip
leash	wharf	chaperon	pitcher

Beginning

Middle

End

Lesson 10
Consonant digraphs sh, th, wh, ch

Write the number of vowels you see in each word. Then write the number of vowel sounds you hear.

Good Work! :)

Vowels

		See	Hear
1.	frame	2	1
2.	cabin	2	2
3.	coat	2	1
4.	deep	2	2
5.	cannot	2	2
6.	beat	2	1
7.	hotel	2	2
8.	feel	2	2
9.	stain	2	(X)1
10.	funny	1	1
11.	visit	2	2
12.	rich	1	1
13.	stand	1	1
14.	read	2	1
15.	basket	2	2
16.	weed	2	2
17.	wild	1	1

Vowels

		See	Hear
18.	animal	3	2
19.	struck	1	1
20.	butterfly	2	(2)1
21.	office	2	2
22.	children	2	2
23.	sleeve	3	2
24.	sentence	3	2
25.	Steve	2	1
26.	music	2	2
27.	Thanksgiving	3	3
28.	roasted	3	(3)2
29.	gently	1	1
30.	cathedral	3	3
31.	something	3	(3)2
32.	colt	1	1
33.	helping	2	2
34.	travel	2	2

Read each word in the word bank. Then write the words in the correct columns according to whether they have one, two, or three syllables.

HINT

If you hear one vowel sound in a word, the word has one syllable. If you hear two vowel sounds in a word, the word has two syllables, and so on.

gymnast	garden	gingerbread	happiness	wild
agent	fence	grocery	children	understand
decide	consonant	cage	splashing	celery
including	radio	desk	guest	post
trace	whale	giraffe	pencil	

One Syllable

_____

_____

_____

_____

_____

_____

_____

Two Syllables

_____

_____

_____

_____

_____

_____

_____

Three Syllables

_____

_____

_____

_____

_____

_____

_____

Here are some titles of songs you may know. Circle each two-syllable word and underline each word with three syllables. Write the two-syllable words on the lines.

1. "Old MacDonald Had a Farm"   **2.** "The Bluebird of Happiness"
3. "The Battle Hymn of the Republic"   **4.** "America, the Beautiful"
5. "Twinkle, Twinkle Little Star"   **6.** "Yankee Doodle Dandy"

_____   _____

_____   _____

_____   _____

Name _____

Reading ▷ Read the interview. Then write your answer to the question at the end of the interview.

Shalini Talks With a Weather Expert

For this month's column, I talked with a weather expert about thunder and lightning.

Q: What causes lightning?

A: Think of a storm cloud as an electricity generator. The positive charge is at the top of the cloud, and the negative charge is at its base. A lightning flash is a spark of electricity between the positive and negative charges. This happens within a cloud, from one cloud to another cloud, or from a cloud to the earth.

Q: Why does lightning often strike trees?

A: When lightning flashes from a cloud to the earth, it takes the easiest path. It is drawn to the highest point in an area, which is often a tree.

Q: What causes thunder?

A: When a lightning flash rushes through the air, it heats up the air molecules along its path. The heated molecules expand and smash into each other. Thunder is the sound made by air molecules crashing together.

Q: Why don't we hear thunder at the same time we see the lightning flash?

A: Light waves travel much faster than sound waves. Light whizzes at 186,000 miles a second! Sound chugs along at about 12 miles a minute. We see a lightning flash at almost the same time it happens, but it takes longer for the sound to reach us.

Where is a dangerous place to be in a thunderstorm? Where *should* you go when you hear thunder?

_____
_____
_____
_____
_____

Review consonant digraphs sh, th, wh, ch; syllables: Reading

 **Writing**

Suppose you are working on a safety campaign in your school. Your task is to prepare a poster with thunderstorm safety tips. List as many tips as you can think of. You may want to finish by making the poster. The words in the word bank may help you.

showers   choice   think   bunch

where   path   should   when

List the most important safety tips first. Keep your sentences short. Use lively, interesting words. Print neatly.

Helpful Hints

Name _____

Read each sentence. Fill in the circle next to the word that correctly completes the sentence. Write the word on the line.

1. Fingerprinting is an important _____ tool.　　○ grocery　○ police

2. Police _____ crime scenes for fingerprints.　　○ dust　○ post

3. _____ do they do this?　　○ Why　○ Who

4. Fingers have patterns of _____.　　○ badges　○ ridges

5. No two people have the same _____.　　○ prints　○ agents

6. People leave prints on things they

　　 _____.　　○ speech　○ touch

7. Police can _____ prints against prints they have on file.　　○ cheer　○ check

8. Fingerprint patterns are either _____, loops, or whorls.　　○ arches　○ inches

9. A plain arch has a wave in the _____.　　○ center　○ cement

10. Loops curve around and _____ out on the same side.　　○ flow　○ flat

11. A _____ consists of ridges that go around and around.　　○ whistle　○ whorl

12. The pattern makes a complete _____.　　○ circle　○ circus

13. To take prints, you need _____ ink.　　○ blank　○ black

14. You also need a printing _____, a roller, and paper.　　○ plate　○ please

15. Press a finger onto an _____ pad.　　○ kind　○ ink

16. Roll each finger onto a _____ card.　　○ test　○ past

Lesson 13

29

Review vowels; hard and soft c, g; blends; digraphs; syllables: Checkup

 Complete each sentence by writing a word from the word bank.

1. Chad and his mom set up the telescope at _____.

2. They set it in _____ on the lawn.

3. Then they looked up at the night _____.

4. The _____ were just appearing.

5. Chad let out a _____ of delight.

6. He _____ his hands loudly.

7. "I see _____!" he shouted.

8. "I can see the rings of Saturn!" he _____.

9. Later, the sky became _____.

10. They _____ back into the house.

sky
place
cried
went
clapped
whoop
cloudy
them
stars
dusk

Read each sentence. Circle the word that correctly completes the sentence. Write it on the line.

11. The _____ on lakes gets thick in winter.　　　ice　　　ink

12. Then people go ice _____.　　　washing　fishing

13. They _____ holes in the ice.　　　dream　drill

14. Some people build _____ there.　　　shacks　shirts

15. Ice fishing is a _____ sport.　　　strange　exchange

16. Ice fishers _____ lines into the water.　　　think　sink

17. _____ they wait for fish to bite.　　　Then　These

18. They _____ a lot of time waiting.　　　stump　spend

19. No one knows _____ they will get lucky.　　　when　while

Review vowels; hard and soft c, g; blends; digraphs; syllables: Checkup

Words with ar, or, er, ir, ur; Sounds of k, f, s; Silent Letters; Syllables

Why is paying attention to details important?

Critical Thinking

> **Study this picture carefully. Then answer the questions without looking at the picture.**

1. What time was it on the bank clock?
2. How many sausages did the dog steal?
3. What were the names of the streets?

4. What was the name on the cart?

5. Which part of the car with the dog inside it was broken?

Home Letter

Dear Family,

In this unit your child will be learning about words that contain the spellings **ar, or, er, ir,** and **ur;** words with the sounds of **k, f,** and **s;** words with silent letters; and syllables.

At-Home Activities

▶ Talk about the picture on page 31. Then have your child choose something on the page to study in detail. After a minute or two, cover the picture and ask your child to write a description of the item, giving as much detail as possible.

▶ Point out the picture of the police officer and Rhoda, the sandwich maker, talking and ask your child what they might be saying. Then act out the scene with one of you playing the police officer and the other playing Rhoda.

▶ Ask your child to draw a picture of a street in your neighborhood. Then make a list together of the things included. Point out any words on the list with the spellings for this unit.

Book Corner

You and your child might enjoy reading these books together.

Sebastian (Super Sleuth) and the Copycat Crime

by Mary Blount Christian

Fans of the clever canine detective will want to join Sebastian on his fast-paced pursuit of the thief.

Stitching Stars—The Story Quilts of Harriet Powers

by Mary Lyons

Harriet Powers' creativity and skill as a quiltmaker are captured in this historical account of her work.

Sincerely,

_____

Name _____

> **Say the name of each picture. Listen for the ar sound as in farm.** If you hear the sound, write the picture name on the line and circle the **ar** in the word.

RULE

The letters **ar** can stand for the vowel sound you hear in **farm.**

1 	2 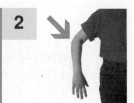	3 	4 
_____	_____	_____	_____
5 	6 	7 	8 
_____	_____	_____	_____

> **Read each sentence. Choose the word from the word bank that correctly completes the sentence and write it on the line.**

9. We read a story about Tony, a palace _____.

10. The best _____ of the story described his job.

11. Tony _____ around the palace each day.

12. The brass buttons on his uniform _____.

13. He unrolled the red _____ for the king.

14. He opened the door of the _____ for the king.

15. He investigated if any _____ rang.

16. He stopped visitors with a wave of his _____.

17. He even tended the royal flower _____.

18. Tony never believed his job was _____.

19. He was proud to keep the king from _____.

sparkled

alarms

guard

harm

carpet

hard

arm

car

marched

garden

part

Markets and Bazaars

Before cars and shopping malls existed, market day was an important weekly event in many parts of the world. Country people carried goods they made or grew to a place in town that was set apart for a market. They bartered their wares for goods they did not have on their farms. One farmer might barter a sackful of carrots for some wool yarn.

Traveling artists came to the market square to entertain the crowds. They often used the bare ground or the back of a cart or wagon for a stage.

Although they are rare in the United States, markets still exist in many other areas. In Asia and North Africa, markets called bazaars can be found in large cities. Along covered streets, shopkeepers and artisans offer food, garments, and all sorts of wares from carpets to glassware. In Arab cities like Baghdad and Cairo, bazaars are permanent markets open every day. Buyers must beware, for the wares sold in a bazaar have no set price. The buyer is expected to bargain with the seller. The smart buyer who can drive a hard bargain gets the best deal!

1. What is the subject of this passage?

_____

2. What word in the passage means "trade by exchanging one kind of good for another"?

_____

3. What did traveling performers use for a stage?

_____

4. What kinds of things are offered for sale in North African bazaars?

_____

What is the difference between paying for things with money and bartering?

Critical Thinking

Name _____

Say the name of each picture. Listen for the **or** sound as in **corn.** If you hear the sound, write the picture name on the line and circle the **or** in the word.

RULE
The letters **or** can stand for the vowel sound you hear in **corn.**

1 	2 	3 	4
5	6 	7 	8 

Read each sentence. Choose the word from the word bank that correctly completes the sentence and write it on the line.

9. This _____ we took a drive.

10. We visited an old _____ town.

11. We drove _____ to reach it.

12. There were many _____ in the town.

13. We bought some violets from a _____.

14. A hospital stood on a street _____.

15. My father said he was _____ there.

16. We saw an old army _____.

17. A _____ was burning in front of it.

18. We heard a musician playing a _____.

19. He was riding a _____ while he played!

corner
horn
morning
horse
fort
torch
north
historical
born
florist
stores

Lesson 15
Words with or

35

Write the word from the word bank that matches each clue. Then read the letters in the shaded boxes to answer the riddle.

organ	dark	tornado	forget	florist
starve	sparkle	artist	explore	forest
alarm	rare	snort	March	orchid

1. opposite of light — — — —

2. feel very hungry — — — — — —

3. month of the year — — — — —

4. sound a pig makes — — — — —

5. exotic flower — — — — — —

6. to shine and glitter — — — — — — —

7. a place to buy flowers — — — — — — —

8. musical instrument — — — — —

9. fail to remember — — — — — —

10. thick woods — — — — — —

11. unusual; seldom found — — — —

12. person who paints or draws — — — — — —

13. frighten — — — — —

14. travel to unknown places — — — — — — —

15. whirling column of air — — — — — — —

What do you call a flavored ape?

_____

Riddle

Name _____

> **Circle the name of each picture. Write the word on the line.**

1

near
north
nurse
first

_____

2

fern
arm
form
firm

_____

3

thirsty
thrifty
thirty
thirteen

_____

4

circle
circus
city
cider

_____

5

toaster
coast
topper
ticket

_____

6

turkey
tricky
trip
turnip

_____

> **Read each sentence. Choose the word from the word bank that correctly completes the sentence and write it on the line.**

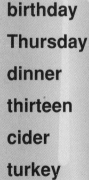

7. Next _____ is a special day for the Dodd family.

8. The twins, Mike and May, will celebrate their

_____.

9. They will be _____ years old that day.

10. Mrs. Dodd will prepare their favorite food for

_____.

11. She will bake a delicious roasted _____.

12. The vegetables will be potatoes and _____.

13. Mr. Dodd will offer his famous apple _____.

14. Cake will be _____ for dessert.

15. After dinner the family will go to the _____.

birthday
Thursday
dinner
thirteen
cider
turkey
turnips
served
circus

Lesson 16
Words with er, ir, ur

37

In each box find the three pictures in a straight or diagonal line whose names have the same vowel sound as **girl.** Draw a line through these pictures.

1.

2.

3.

4.

Name _____

Virginia	printer	stirs
furniture	whirl	churn
cider	preserved	experts
curls	church	purple
Governor's	serve	

1. Williamsburg is a colonial town in _____ .

2. The town, its streets, and its homes are well _____ .

3. An old _____ with a steeple stands as it did in the past.

4. Craftspeople make colonial _____ .

5. A _____ shows how books were made long ago.

6. A woman _____ hot wax to make candles.

7. The candles are colored red and _____ .

8. Other people in colonial costumes make butter in a
   _____ .

9. Restaurants _____ traditional colonial meals.

10. Delicious apple _____ is on every menu.

11. The tour guides are _____ in American history.

12. Street dancers _____ past the curious crowds.

13. The _____ Mansion is a popular attraction.

14. Smoke _____ from its huge brick chimney.

What do people learn from historical places like Williamsburg?

Critical Thinking

Read each word. Circle each word in which er, ir, or, or ur follows Long Vowel Rule 1.

1. snore
2. cures
3. work
4. firm
5. floor
6. thirty
7. burr
8. core
9. hire
10. worm
11. severe
12. score
13. door
14. purr
15. retire
16. spire
17. her
18. more
19. tires
20. very
21. stir
22. lure
23. cord
24. fur
25. store

 Read each clue. Find the word above that matches the clue. Write the word in the crossword puzzle.

Across

1. a thick string
3. these are found on a car or bike
6. greater in number
8. part of a church
9. to attract with bait
10. an opening in a wall
12. to pay someone to do a job
13. a sound made while sleeping
14. the part of a room to walk on

Down

1. the center of an apple
2. to move around
4. teams' points
5. strict or harsh
7. a doctor helps find these
8. a place of business where things are bought and sold
11. to give up a job

Name _____

 **Reading** ▶ **Read the passage. Then write your answer to the question at the end of the passage.**

GROWING UP AMISH

Amish people immigrated here from Switzerland and Germany more than 250 years ago. They were searching for a country where they would be free to follow their religious beliefs. Amish people who follow church rules strictly do not drive cars or use modern farm equipment. They travel by horse-drawn carriage and use horses to pull their plows and carts. They do not have electricity or telephones in their homes.

Amish boys and men wear long black pants, dark shirts, and straw hats. Girls and women wear long solid-color dresses. Starched white caps cover their hair.

In Amish farming communities, young children help plant and weed the vegetable gardens. Older children do chores such as feeding the horses, hogs, and chickens. When crops are planted and harvested, everyone shares the hard work.

Social gatherings in Amish farming communities center on farm activities, such as cornhusking. When a newly married couple needs a barn or a church member's barn has burned down in a fire, the whole community gathers to help build a new barn. Barn raising—in addition to work—is a time for playing, talking, singing, and being together.

What are some of the differences between the Amish way of life and your way of life?

_____
_____
_____
_____
_____

Writing

Imagine that you have an opportunity to spend a day on an Amish farm. Write a journal entry telling about your day. Use some of the words from the word bank. Here are some details you might want to remember.

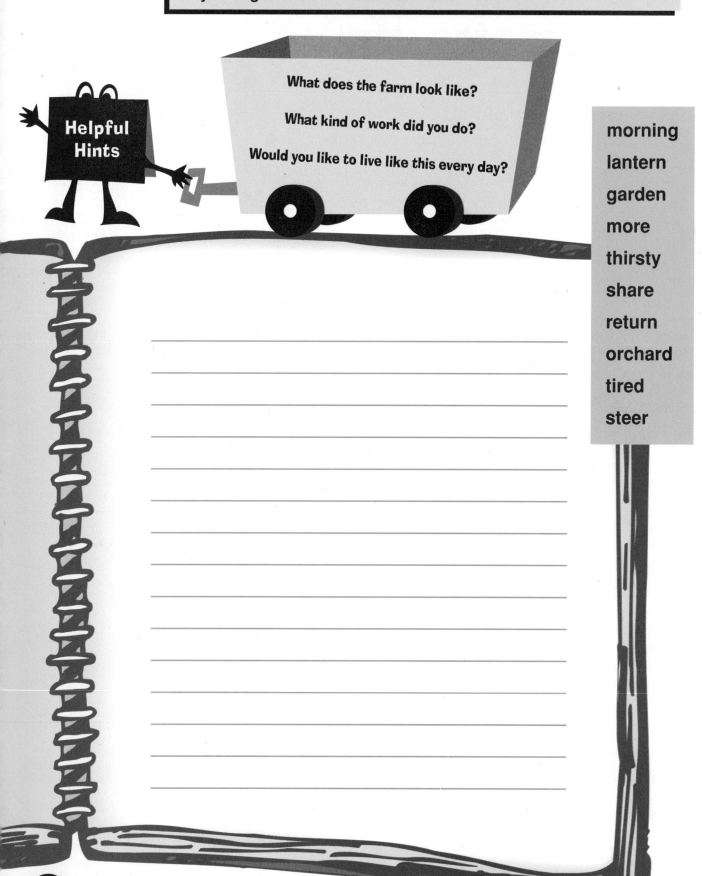

Helpful Hints

What does the farm look like?

What kind of work did you do?

Would you like to live like this every day?

morning
lantern
garden
more
thirsty
share
return
orchard
tired
steer

Say the name of each picture and listen for the **k** sound. Fill in the first, middle, or last circle to show whether the sound of **k** comes at the beginning, middle, or end of the word.

DEFINITION

The letters **k** and **ck** stand for the sound **k**. If the letter **c** comes before the letters **a, o,** or **u,** it stands for the **k** sound.

kitten   pi**ck**   **c**an

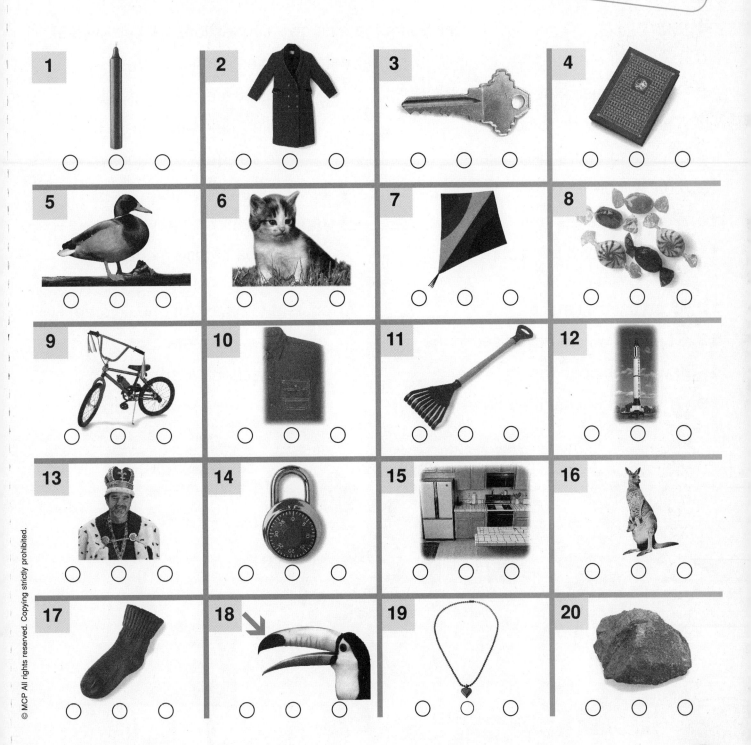

Lesson 19
Words with the k sound
43

Read each sentence. Complete the sentence by writing the word in parentheses that has the **k** sound. Then circle the letter or letters that stand for the **k** sound.

1. The girls' soccer team is _____ plans for a fund-raiser. (arranging, making)

2. Ms. Garcia, their _____ , is helping. (coach, sponsor)

3. Jennie, the team _____ , is taking notes. (leader, captain)

4. She _____ notes as the girls give suggestions. (takes, writes)

5. Later, Jennie _____ her notes. (copies, more)

6. The team uses them to _____ the best idea. (choose, pick)

7. The team votes to hold a _____ sale. (bake, pie)

8. Nicki and Laura will make _____ to sell. (cheese, cookies)

9. Loni will prepare _____ whipped-cream pies. (rich, thick)

10. Peg will operate the _____ register. (cash, change)

11. Ms. Garcia will bring paper _____ for the customers. (sacks, bags)

12. Everyone will make _____ posters to hang. (bright, colored)

13. The sale will be advertised in the _____ papers. (town, local)

14. It will be held in the _____ near the school. (park, yard)

15. The team will set up a huge _____ there. (canopy, tent)

What is the main idea of this story?

Critical Thinking

Name _____

Read each sentence. Underline the words that contain ch. Then write the words in the correct columns.

1. Twenty children were chosen to attend a school assembly.

2. Each one sits in a chair in front of a chalkboard.

3. The schedule shows the order of the speakers on a chart.

4. An architect who designs kitchens goes first.

5. An orchestra leader and a choral director speak next.

6. A chemist, a mechanic, and a chemistry teacher speak last.

ch as in school

_____ _____
_____ _____
_____ _____
_____ _____

ch as in church

_____ _____
_____ _____
_____ _____
_____ _____

Read each sentence. Choose the word from the word bank that correctly completes the sentence and write it on the line.

7. We went to an _____ shop that sold interesting, old things.

8. We found many one-of-a-kind, or _____, items.

9. Some were made with _____ seldom used today.

10. There was not one _____ item in the shop!

unique

techniques

grotesque

antique

RULE

The letters **qu** stand for the **kw** sound.

quote   **qu**ick   **qu**ilt

As you read, think about why an audience applauds at the end of a performance.

Critical Thinking

1. My dad took me to listen to a symphony _____ from Russia.

2. They performed in the high _____ auditorium.

3. As the lights dimmed, the audience became very

   _____ .

4. Everyone applauded when the orchestra's _____ walked onto the stage.

5. I enjoyed watching the violinists as they _____ the strings on their violins.

6. One musician had a _____ instrument that was unlike any other in the world.

7. The orchestra was joined by a famous pianist whose

   fingers breezed along the piano _____ .

8. His playing _____ was perfect.

9. The sounds of the final chords _____ through the concert hall.

10. The audience _____ jumped to its feet to applaud.

quiet
conductor
quickly
keys
plucked
echoed
unique
technique
orchestra
school

Name

 Say each word. Underline the letters that stand for the f sound. Then write the words under the correct headings.

RULE

The letters **ph** and **gh** can stand for the **f** sound.

dol**ph**in   lau**gh**

feathers	enough	
phones	cough	fine
photo	telegraph	phony
feature	typhoon	digraph
triumph	phonics	fail
orphan	Philip	pamphlet
fingers	graph	tough
telephone	furniture	laugh
rough	finish	nephew
typhoid	sulphur	

ph

_____   _____   _____

_____   _____   _____

_____   _____   _____

_____   _____   _____

_____

gh

_____   _____   _____

_____   _____

f

_____   _____   _____

_____   _____   _____

_____

THE FANTASTIC FROG

A frog in a city, it just can't be true.
It must be a phantom or a statue.
A dolphin perhaps, or an elephant maybe.
But how could a frog in a city be happy?
But look! There is Philip, in his suit and tie,
Looking quite smart and not a bit shy.
Reading the papers is one of his crazes.
Finding the meaning from paragraphs and phrases.
He uses the phone like a city tycoon.
And rushes around like a wild typhoon,
Shopping in big stores and riding in autos,
Watching the people and taking some photos.
When asked why he left his home in the pool,
He laughed as he said, "Well, I'm not a fool.
The water was wet and the going was rough.
To tell you quite frankly, I'd had quite enough."
His biography will be read with amazement,
For a frog out of water—that's quite an achievement!

Is this poem fantasy or reality? How can you tell?

Critical Thinking

1. Philip is a _____. (elephant, dolphin, frog)

2. He rushes around like a _____. (phantom, hyphen, typhoon)

3. When asked why he left the pool, Philip _____.
(laughed, coughed, phoned)

4. His _____ will be read with amazement.
(pamphlet, biography, phonograph)

Name

RULE

The letter **s** can stand for the **s, z,** or **sh** sounds

safe   rose   sure

1. A tired sea lion swam surely through the water toward the beach.
2. The powerful waves helped push it onto the land.
3. The sea lion closed its weary eyes and went to sleep.
4. Rosa and her father were walking on the beach when they saw the sea lion.
5. "Does it need help, Dad?" Rosa asked her father.
6. "Is it sick? Do we need to get help for it?"
7. "I'm not sure," her dad said, looking the sea lion over.
8. "We need to observe it for awhile."
9. "That way we can assure ourselves about it."
10. When it heard them, the sea lion raised its head and opened its eyes.
11. That reassured Rosa, who had been very worried.
12. Suddenly the sea lion gave a noisy bark and swam off.

s as in safe	s as in rose	s as in sure

Read each sentence. Then look at the pictures. In the box under each picture, write the number of the sentence that matches it. Underline each word in which **s** stands for the **z** sound. Circle each word in which **s** stands for the **sh** sound.

1. We rose early on the farm.
2. After rising, we ate breakfast.
3. Andy served oatmeal with sugar .
4. Then we began our chores.
5. Sam raked the fallen leaves.
6. Cousin Rosie fed the cows.
7. Esther pruned the roses.
8. The morning surely flew!

Read each sentence and draw a picture of it in the box. Then circle the words in the sentence that have a silent gh.

HINT

Sometimes the letters **gh** are silent and do not have any sound.

fou*gh*t

1. Our neighbor's daughter brought us a fish she had caught.

2. They sought the naughty cat and found him in the bough of a mighty tree.

3. The flight of the airplane took it high over the mighty Rocky Mountains.

4. We weighed the dough and made eight pizzas right there.

RULE

The letters **rh** stand for the **r** sound. The **h** is silent.

rhythm

Rhode Island   rhymes   rhino

rhubarb   rhododendron

1. Tara loves to visit her grandmother in _____ .

2. She and Tara work outside, tending the flowering _____ bushes.

3. In the cool evenings they make _____ pies.

4. As they work, they make up silly _____ .

5. The one about a huge gray _____ really made them laugh.

Read each sentence. Choose the word from the word bank that correctly completes the sentence and write it on the line.

RULE

The letters **wr** stand for the **r** sound. The **w** is silent.

wring

wrong   wreck   wrist   wrestle   wrap

6. The boys are learning to _____ in gym class.

7. The coach cautions against making a _____ move.

8. Moving incorrectly could result in an injured _____ .

9. It could also _____ the muscles in a knee.

10. Some boys _____ their knees with an elastic bandage for extra support.

Name _____

Read each sentence. Choose the word from the word bank that correctly completes the sentence and write it on the line.

RULE

The letters **gn** and **kn** stand for the **n** sound. The **g** and the **k** are silent.

gnaw **kn**ew

gnarled

know

knotholes

knickers

gnome

knee

knight

1. Sir Lance, a brave _____, rides to a forest.

2. The forest is filled with old _____ trees.

3. Legend says that a tiny _____ lives in one tree.

4. This creature is no taller than your _____.

5. He dresses in plaid _____ and a red vest.

6. Lance is anxious to get to _____ this elf.

7. Lance searches in the _____ of every tree.

Read each sentence. Choose the word from the word bank that correctly completes the sentence and write it on the line.

RULE

The letters **sc** and **st** will sometimes stand for the **s** sound. The **c** and the **t** are silent.

scene li**st**en

glistened   hastened   scenic

scent   muscles   whistle

8. The thief escaped into the _____ village.

9. The police _____ to inform the villagers.

10. With a loud _____ the dogs were called.

11. The dogs picked up the _____ of the thief.

12. With powerful _____ the dogs chased him.

13. Later, handcuffs _____ on the thief's wrists.

1. knee   **2.** gnome   **3.** whistled   **4.** knoll

5. muscles   **6.** knuckles   **7.** gnarled   **8.** scenery

9. knew   **10.** descended   **11.** sign   **12.** knapsacks

13. gnawing   **14.** scenic   **15.** glistened   **16.** know

Read each sentence and complete it with the correct word from above.

17. There was no _____ of rain when Fern and Carla woke up.

18. They decided to climb a nearby _____.

19. The girls buckled on their _____.

20. Carla _____ a tune as they walked.

21. "I _____ this hike was a good idea!" Fern said.

22. At the top of the hill, they admired the _____.

23. Sunlight _____ off a small pond.

24. A beaver was _____ on a young tree.

25. "What a _____ view!" Fern exclaimed.

26. "Yes, but my _____ is hurting," Carla said.

27. "I'm going to rest by this _____ old tree."

28. "My _____ are a little sore, too," said Fern.

29. Fern knocked her _____ against the tree.

30. "It's hollow! I wonder if a _____ lives in it," she said.

31. "I guess we'll never _____," Carla said.

32. Then the two girls _____ the hill and went home.

Name _____

Read each word. Write the number of vowels you see in each word. Then write the number of vowel sounds you hear.

Vowels

	See	Hear
1. furniture	_____	_____
2. candle	_____	_____
3. pose	_____	_____
4. rough	_____	_____
5. liquid	_____	_____
6. kite	_____	_____
7. cough	_____	_____
8. campaign	_____	_____
9. cabbage	_____	_____
10. scientist	_____	_____
11. quote	_____	_____
12. gnome	_____	_____
13. knell	_____	_____
14. locket	_____	_____
15. weigh	_____	_____
16. typhoid	_____	_____
17. enough	_____	_____
18. gnarl	_____	_____

Vowels

	See	Hear
19. wrangler	_____	_____
20. comical	_____	_____
21. neighbor	_____	_____
22. insurance	_____	_____
23. antique	_____	_____
24. boughs	_____	_____
25. quail	_____	_____
26. cyclone	_____	_____
27. ache	_____	_____
28. daughter	_____	_____
29. chorus	_____	_____
30. queen	_____	_____
31. phone	_____	_____
32. banquet	_____	_____
33. knuckle	_____	_____
34. architect	_____	_____
35. photograph	_____	_____
36. rhinoceros	_____	_____

1. telephone _____   2. insect _____

3. glisten _____   4. quiz _____

5. magazine _____   6. mechanic _____

7. Philip _____   8. wrist _____

9. campaign _____   10. cough _____

11. locket _____   12. antique _____

13. rhubarb _____   14. tissue _____

15. wise _____   16. candy _____

17. king _____   18. jacket _____

19. kangaroo _____   20. rhythm _____

21. sign _____   22. wrangler _____

23. biography _____   24. whisper _____

25. husband _____   26. science _____

27. basement _____   28. rake _____

29. wrong _____   30. phonograph _____

31. rhinoceros _____   32. cousin _____

33. typhoon _____   34. elephant _____

35. phantom _____   36. positive _____

37. wreck _____   38. knapsack _____

39. photo _____   40. kitchen _____

41. chorus _____   42. equal _____

43. block _____   44. digraph _____

45. answer _____   46. sugar _____

47. fight _____   48. knoll _____

49. treasure _____   50. gnome _____

Reading ▶ Read the folk tale. Then write your answer to the question at the end of the folk tale.

COYOTE'S PRESENT

Coyote was walking with Spider when they saw a unique rock. "This fine rock looks cold," said Coyote. "I'll give it my blanket." Coyote wrapped his thick blanket around the rock. "Here is a present for you," Coyote said.

The two friends walked on, whistling a tune. Soon a cold rain began to fall. Coyote began to cough. "Spider, please go back and get my blanket," Coyote begged. Spider hastened back to the rock. "My friend Coyote needs his blanket," he said. The rock refused to give back the blanket. "What's given is given," it said.

When Spider told this to Coyote, Coyote became angry. He hastened back to the rock. "I'm sure I need this more than you do," he told the rock as he wrapped himself in the blanket.

Suddenly, Coyote and Spider heard a frightening sound. The rock was rolling after them! They ran as quickly as they could, but the rock rolled right over them and snatched up the blanket, saying, "What's given is given."

Coyote picked himself up. "I know now I was wrong," he decided. "If you give someone a present, you give it forever."

{ **W**hat lesson did Coyote learn?

_____
_____
_____
_____

Writing

In Native American folk tales, Coyote is always getting into trouble! Write your own folk tale about a lesson Coyote learns. Use the words in the word bank. Here are some things to think about before you write.

phony	wreck	scene
quickly	tough	gnarled
treasure	muscles	know
	rhythm	

Where does your story take place?
Who are the characters?
What do they do?

Helpful Hints

Name _____

1. Rhoda is learning to use a video _____.

    camera   cough
    ○   ○

2. She wants to create _____ films.

    unique   physique
    ○   ○

3. The camera does not _____ much.

    rough   weigh
    ○   ○

4. She does not need strong _____ to carry it.

    thistles   muscles
    ○   ○

5. Rhoda _____ a lot about filmmaking.

    knows   knees
    ○   ○

6. She answers all my _____.

    quick   questions
    ○   ○

7. We are _____ the script together.

    writing   wrong
    ○   ○

8. The title is "The Phony _____."

    Hyphen   Phantom
    ○   ○

9. The film features an evil _____.

    chemist   chorus
    ○   ○

10. He always talks in _____.

    rhinos   rhymes
    ○   ○

11. The story starts with a _____.

    short   storm
    ○   ○

12. A _____ burns up the chemist's lab.

    fire   first
    ○   ○

13. My _____ Hugh and I will act in Rhoda's film.

    naughty   neighbor
    ○   ○

14. We will also design the _____.

    scenery   scents
    ○   ○

15. We are _____ our film will be great!

    sugar   sure
    ○   ○

16. Someday Rhoda will be a famous _____.

    stir   star
    ○   ○

 Read each sentence. Think about the way the underlined words are related. Then choose one of the words in the word bank to complete the sentence.

rhubarb	wrong	rough	whistle	quack	herd
kitchen	thirsty	gnaw	rose	scent	fur
elephant	knee	antique	ghost	sugar	chorus

1. Nice is to naughty as right is to _____.

2. Car is to garage as stove is to _____.

3. Quill is to porcupine as _____ is to cat.

4. Nose is to person as trunk is to _____.

5. Elbow is to arm as _____ is to leg.

6. Dolphin is to animal as _____ is to plant.

7. Rare is to unique as old is to _____.

8. Purr is to cat as _____ is to duck.

9. Sour is to lemon as sweet is to _____.

10. Gnome is to elf as phantom is to _____.

11. Wreck is to smash as _____ is to chew.

12. Hungry is to eat as _____ is to drink.

13. Orange is to fruit as _____ is to flower.

14. Forget is to remember as smooth is to _____.

15. Play is to orchestra as sing is to _____.

16. Sound is to noise as _____ is to odor.

17. Beat is to drum as blow is to _____.

18. Flock is to birds as _____ is to deer.

MEMO

TO: Agent 4U3

FROM:

UR A MENT IS 2 W8 LY AT THE . AGENT

6U6 WILL B A FULL OF IM   S. U R

 ABLE OF 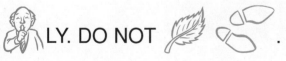 ING 6U6. DO NOT  ED.

STAY  FUL AND W8

 LY. DO NOT 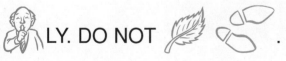 .

This message uses pictures, letters, and numbers to stand for words. Which of the coded words did you have the most trouble reading? Can you think of a different way to represent that word?

Critical Thinking

▶ Decode the secret message.

Home Letter

Dear Family,

The focus of our work over the next few weeks will be on suffixes: word endings such as **-s, -ed, -ing, -less, -ful, -ment,** and **-ness,** and the spelling changes that may take place when suffixes are added to base words.

At-Home Activities

▶ Have your child read the coded message on the other side of this letter to you. Point out the words with suffixes that are used in the message (night**ly**, help**ing**, tir**ed**, paper**s**, quiet**ly**, watch**ful**).

▶ Have your child look for words with suffixes in other reading materials, such as newspapers and magazines. Help your child figure out the meanings of the words.

▶ Take turns with your child writing coded messages to one another. You might place your messages on a bulletin board or the refrigerator. Try to use words with suffixes in your messages.

Book Corner

You and your child might enjoy reading these books together. Look for them in your local library.

What Eric Knew: A Sebastian Barth Mystery
by James Howe

A note to Sebastian with only "S.I.S." printed on it launches a mystery that has the popular sleuth—and readers—sifting through many clues.

Math Mini-Mysteries
by Sandra Markle

Through this book's fun-to-do projects and clever examples, learn the secrets of how to use mathematics for solving many mysteries.

Sincerely,

Name _____

DEFINITION
The word to which a suffix is added is called the **base word.**

	s	**ed**	**ing**
1. cook	_____	_____	_____
2. learn	_____	_____	_____
3. work	_____	_____	_____
4. clean	_____	_____	_____
5. pick	_____	_____	_____
6. help	_____	_____	_____
7. shiver	_____	_____	_____
8. disturb	_____	_____	_____

Write the base word for each word.

9. walks	_____	**10.** covered	_____
11. guessed	_____	**12.** frightens	_____
13. talking	_____	**14.** lifts	_____
15. hitched	_____	**16.** cleaned	_____
17. buys	_____	**18.** raining	_____
19. rolling	_____	**20.** loves	_____
21. packed	_____	**22.** burned	_____
23. spelling	_____	**24.** picking	_____

RULE

When **ed** is added to a base word ending in **d** or **t,** it stands for the **ed** sound. Other times **ed** will stand for the sound of **d** or **t.**

They plant**ed** a tree.

He cheer**ed** for the team.

She jump**ed** over the rope.

1. learned _____
2. heaped _____
3. squirted _____
4. walked _____
5. shirked _____
6. fixed _____
7. served _____
8. scalded _____

9. called _____
10. rushed _____
11. carted _____
12. asked _____
13. planted _____
14. finished _____
15. turned _____
16. searched _____

17. hunted _____
18. handed _____

Read each sentence. Circle the word that correctly completes the sentence and write it on the line.

19. Last summer we _____ to California.

tripped
climbed
traveled

20. We _____ on a warm, sunny morning.

departed
fixed
asked

21. My brother was _____ next to me.

seated
moaned
risked

22. I _____ him if I could sit by the window.

planted
blinked
asked

23. The airplane _____ off smoothly.

loaned
lifted
hatched

Name _____

> **Read each sentence. Underline each word that is used to compare two things. Circle each word that is used to compare more than two things.**

RULE

The suffix **er** is added to words to compare two things. The suffix **est** is added to words to compare more than two things.

My jacket is **warm**.

My coat is **warmer**.

My winter parka is the **warmest** of all.

1. This winter went faster than last winter.

2. It is because the weather was nicer.

3. We had the warmest winter in ten years.

4. Temperatures were much higher than usual.

5. Some days were warmer than others.

6. Precipitation was lighter than usual.

7. Last year the winter wind was stronger.

8. That wind was the wildest I have ever seen.

9. It brought the lowest temperatures ever.

> **Add the suffixes er and est to form new words.**

	er	**est**
10. clear	_____	_____
11. dark	_____	_____
12. low	_____	_____
13. young	_____	_____
14. short	_____	_____
15. bright	_____	_____
16. narrow	_____	_____
17. smooth	_____	_____
18. dull	_____	_____
19. rough	_____	_____

1. We have the _____ class of all! (great)

2. Joe is the _____ runner in the class. (fast)

3. He is even _____ than Rodney. (fast)

4. Pamela gets the _____ grades of all. (high)

5. She has the _____ writing in the class. (neat)

6. I am the _____ student in the school. (tall)

7. Even Mr. Stevens is _____ than I am! (short)

8. Mr. Stevens is _____ than your teacher. (funny)

9. He tells the _____ jokes I've ever heard. (funny)

10. I always laugh the _____ of all. (loud)

11. the age of two people

Sam is older than Gretchen. _____

_____

12. the height of three trees

_____

_____

13. the size of two boxes

_____

_____

14. the length of three baseball bats

_____

_____

Form new words by adding the correct suffixes.
Write the new words on the lines.

RULE

When a word ends in silent **e**, drop the **e** before adding a suffix that begins with a vowel.

save + **s** = **saves**   save + **ed** = **saved**
save + **ing** = **saving**   nice + **er** = **nicer**
nice = **est** = **nicest**

E COMING SOON

s   **ed**   **ing**

1. pave

2. tease

3. blame

4. describe

5. divide

6. wave

er   **est**

7. late

8. grave

9. fine

10. cute

11. polite

12. crude

Write the base word for each word.

13. skating _____   14. glides _____

15. traced _____   16. hugest _____

17. grazing _____   18. later _____

> **Form a new word by putting each base word and suffix together. Write the new word on the line.**

1. dive + ing _____

2. wave + ing _____

3. late + est _____

4. smile + ing _____

5. wade + ed _____

6. leave + ing _____

7. come + ing _____

8. loose + er _____

9. love + ed _____

10. wise + er _____

11. grade + ed _____

12. nice + er _____

13. cute + est _____

14. face + ing _____

> **Complete each sentence with one of the new words you formed above.**

15. Let's watch the videotape of our _____ day at the beach.

16. Here we are _____ up the walkway.

17. Everyone is smiling and _____ their hands at the camera.

18. Joe is the one not _____ the camera.

19. Beth really has the _____ smile of all of us!

20. Is this part of the _____ contest?

21. This is when Mom _____ with Beth in the shallow water.

22. Here we are getting into the car and _____ for home.

23. We all certainly _____ that day at the beach!

24. It was _____ than the last time we went.

Name _____

Circle each word that ends in a single consonant. Then add the suffixes to make new words.

When a one-syllable short-vowel word ends in a single consonant, double the consonant before adding a suffix that begins with a vowel.

slip   slipped   slipping

ed

ing

1. fit _____   _____

2. act _____   _____

3. wrap _____   _____

4. rest _____   _____

5. blot _____   _____

6. knit _____   _____

er

est

7. fat _____   _____

8. fond _____   _____

9. mad _____   _____

10. hot _____   _____

11. cold _____   _____

12. sad _____   _____

Circle each word with a suffix and write its base word on the line.

13. Our cat, Alex, washed his fur. _____

14. Then he wrapped himself into a ball. _____

15. Alex lay on the windowsill and napped. _____

16. He will be resting until bedtime! _____

Words that double the final consonant to add a suffix

RULE

When a one syllable short-vowel word ends in a single consonant, double the consonant before adding a suffix that begins with a vowel.

ma**d**   ma**dder**   ma**ddest**

1. slim + er _____

2. flat + er _____

3. bold + est _____

4. run + ing _____

5. grin + ed _____

6. scrub + ed _____

7. drip + ing _____

8. plot + ed _____

9. swim + ing _____

10. hot + est _____

11. set + ing _____

12. hug + ed _____

Complete each sentence with one of the new words you formed above. Then circle the base word in the word you wrote.

13. Diane, an explorer, was _____ out on an exciting trip.

14. On the _____ day of the summer, she departed.

15. She had _____ her course on a map.

16. Diane would be _____ along trails part of the time.

17. She would move easily over the _____ terrain.

18. When she reached the river, she would do some _____ .

19. The sun would quickly dry her wet and _____ clothes.

20. Diane _____ her parents before leaving.

21. She _____ happily as she waved goodbye.

Name _____

Form new words by adding the suffix y to the base words. Write the new words on the lines.

When a word ends in silent **e**, drop the **e** before adding **y**. When a word ends in a single consonant preceded by a short-vowel sound, double the consonant before adding **y**.

i**ce** + **y** = **icy**   fo**g** + **y** = **foggy**

1. crab _____

2. luck _____

3. spice _____

4. edge _____

5. haste _____   8. rose _____

6. chill _____   9. noise _____

7. flop _____   10. smog _____

Read each sentence. Complete the sentence by adding ly to the correct word in the word bank. Write the new word on the line.

The suffix **ly** can be added to many words to form a word that tells how.

soft + **ly** = **softly**

11. Dana and Tad's baby-sitting business is

_____ becoming a success.

12. They take their job _____ .

13. They look forward _____ to the children's arrival.

14. When the baby naps, Tad asks the others not

to play _____ .

15. Dana also tells the children to talk _____ .

16. Before they go home, the children must put away their toys

_____ .

glad
loud
slow
quiet
serious
neat

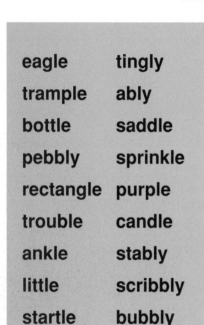

RULE

When **ly** is added to a word ending in **le**, the **le** is dropped.

nimb**le** + **ly** = nimbly

feeb**le** + **ly** = feebly

Word Bank

eagle	tingly
trample	ably
bottle	saddle
pebbly	sprinkle
rectangle	purple
trouble	candle
ankle	stably
little	scribbly
startle	bubbly

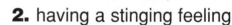

Across

1. container for liquids
4. to surprise
7. a worry or a difficulty
8. having stones worn smooth and round
14. a flat figure with four sides and four right angles
16. the joint that connects the foot and the leg
17. doing something well

Down

2. having a stinging feeling
3. small in size
4. in a steady way
5. to tread or step hard on
6. a stick of wax with a wick that gives light when burned
9. having bubbles
10. to scatter drops or bits
11. a mixture of red and blue
12. written carelessly
13. a large strong bird
15. a padded seat on a horse

Form a new word by combining each base word and suffix. Write the new word on the line.

RULE

If a word ends in **y** preceded by a consonant, change the **y** to **i** and add **es, ed,** or **ly.** Do not change the **y** to **i** when adding the suffix **ing** or when adding **ly** to a one-syllable word that ends in **y** preceded by a consonant. If a word ends in **y** preceded by a vowel, just add the suffix.

cry + **es** = **cries**

cry + **ed** = **cried**

happy + **ly** = **happily**

cry + **ing** = **crying**

dry + **ly** = **dryly**

enjoy + **s** = **enjoys**

1. fly + es _____

2. employ + s _____

3. dirty + er _____

4. coy + ly _____

5. fly + ing _____

6. clumsy + ly _____

7. study + ed _____

8. sly + ly _____

9. curl + er _____

10. reply + ed _____

Read each sentence. Underline each word with a suffix added to a base word that ends in y. Then write the base word on the line.

11. We were all studying together at the library. _____

12. Helen multiplied numbers on her calculator. _____

13. Tomás copied his rough draft. _____

14. I shyly asked a librarian for help. _____

15. The librarian said he enjoyed helping me. _____

16. Luckily he found the book I needed. _____

Form new words by adding suffixes to base words. Write the words on the lines.

	s/es	**ed**	**ing**
cry	1. _____	_____	_____
enjoy	2. _____	_____	_____
reply	3. _____	_____	_____
carry	4. _____	_____	_____
play	5. _____	_____	_____
study	6. _____	_____	_____

	er	**est**	**ly**
clumsy	7. _____	_____	_____
easy	8. _____	_____	_____
lucky	9. _____	_____	_____
sly	10. _____	_____	_____
scary	11. _____	_____	_____
heavy	12. _____	_____	_____

Read the passage. Underline words with y that have had suffixes added.

In the 1700s, ladies often wore straw bonnets. These were imported from other countries because they could not be made easily at home. Then a woman named Betsey Metcalf invented an easier way of braiding the straw. She taught her method to many women employed in bonnet making. Because she never applied for a patent, however, she couldn't profit from her discovery.

Name _____

> ▶ **Circle the suffix in each word.**

1. payment
2. needless
3. gladness
4. statement
5. hopeful
6. fearless
7. thankful
8. greatness
9. mindful
10. goodness
11. darkness
12. government
13. restful
14. fairness
15. shipment
16. development

> ▶ **Form a new word by putting each base word and suffix together. Write the new word on the line. Then use the words you wrote to complete the sentences below.**

17. equip + ment _____
18. help + ful _____
19. color + ful _____
20. spot + less _____
21. cold + ness _____
22. assign + ment _____
23. cheer + ful _____
24. hope + less _____
25. fear + less _____
26. kind + ness _____
27. bright + ness _____
28. enjoy + ment _____

29. The newly fallen snow raised my spirits
    and made me _____.

30. The _____ of the sunlight
    on the snow hurt my eyes.

31. The _____ of the air nipped my nose.

32. I had my ski _____ with me.

33. The ski instructor gave me some
    _____ tips.

34. I was _____ as I skied down the hill.

35. When I got to the bottom, my _____
    was complete.

Form a new word by putting the base word and suffix together. Write the new word on the line. Remember the rules for adding suffixes.

1. pass + age _____
2. beat + able _____
3. enjoy + able _____
4. avail + able _____
5. disturb + ance _____
6. remit + ance _____
7. bag + age _____
8. short + age _____

Read each sentence. Complete the sentence by adding able, age, or ance to a base word in the word bank. Write the new word on the line.

9. We carried the _____ to the post office.

10. The clerk asked, "May I be of _____?"

11. We wanted to know if the box was _____ for mailing.

12. We asked how much _____ was needed to mail it.

13. The clerk stamped "delicate" on the box because the contents were _____ .

14. "Are the contents _____ to you?" asked the clerk.

15. "You might want to buy _____ if they're worth a lot."

16. "You can buy it for a _____ cost."

post	value
insure	assist
break	accept
pack	reason

Name _____

▶ **Form a new word by putting the base word and suffix together. Write the new word on the line.**

RULE

The suffixes **en, ity, ive,** and **some** change the way a base word is used.

gold + **en** = **golden** (to make or become like gold)

humid + **ity** = **humidity** (the quality of being humid)

act + **ive** = **active** (full of action)

lone + **some** = **lonesome** (having a lonely feeling)

1. detect + ive _____

2. whole + some _____

3. sad + en _____

4. disrupt + ive _____

5. tire + some _____

6. sharp + en _____

7. national + ity _____

8. universe + ity _____

▶ **Read each sentence and find the picture that goes with it. Write the number of the sentence on the line under the picture. Then circle each word that contains ity, en, ive, or some.**

9. The massive hot-air balloon was awesome.

10. The broken lamp suggested the possibility of foul play.

11. The speaker was impressive and not tiresome.

12. The quarrelsome cat jumped on the wooden box.

13. The creative artist painted an impressive golden sun.

_____   _____   _____   _____

RULE

Often the suffixes **ion, tion,** and **sion** are added to base words. These suffixes mean **the act, condition,** or **result of something**.

correct + **ion** = correction

precise + **sion** = precision

create + **tion** = creation

1. The students at Oak Park School receive a fine _____.

2. First graders learn to listen to a _____ from the teacher.

3. Fourth graders learn to solve _____ problems.

4. Sixth graders will have a _____ about the government.

5. They will see a film about voting in the _____ of a president.

6. The film will be shown on _____.

7. In science, fifth graders read about _____.

8. Some students are doing a report on the _____ of animals.

9. They will write a _____ of their rough draft.

10. The students work hard until summer _____.

How is Oak Park School like your school? How is it different?

Critical Thinking

education	direction
discussion	subtraction
protection	collision
operation	pollution
election	television
revision	vacation

Read the sentence in each box. Draw a picture to show what the sentence means. Then circle the words in the sentence that have the suffix **ward**.

The suffix **ward** means **in the direction of** or **toward**.

back + **ward** = **backward** (toward the back)

home + **ward** = **homeward** (in the direction of home)

1. Kurt looked upward and saw a colorful balloon drifting toward him.

2. Mother stopped the car from rolling backward down the hill.

3. The hikers carefully climbed downward from the top of the mountain.

4. The band marched forward, toward the center of town.

1. carefully
2. sharpened
3. seemingly
4. surprisingly
5. alarmingly
6. frightening
7. cheerfulness
8. heartened
9. saddened
10. handsomely
11. actively
12. flattened
13. acceptances
14. defensively
15. enjoyably

 Read each sentence. Underline the word with more than one suffix. Then write the base word on the line.

16. Our trip to the museum went surprisingly quickly.

_____

17. We appreciated the thoughtfulness of our guide.

_____

18. The guide told us to study the exhibits carefully.

_____

19. The dinosaur exhibit was attractively displayed.

_____

20. Some of the skeletons were alarmingly huge.

_____

21. A live mammoth would have been frightening.

_____

22. The guide involved us actively in discussions.

_____

23. He cheerfully answered all our questions.

_____

24. We were saddened when it was time to leave.

_____

For each word, write the number of vowels you see, the number of vowel sounds you hear, and the number of syllables.

RULE

A suffix is a syllable in itself if it contains a vowel sound.

	Vowels You See	Vowel Sounds You Hear	Syllables		Vowels You See	Vowel Sounds You Hear	Syllables
cloudy	___	___	___	curly	___	___	___
carrier	___	___	___	happiness	___	___	___
cheer	___	___	___	sleepier	___	___	___
fanciest	___	___	___	heavily	___	___	___
pities	___	___	___	handsome	___	___	___
available	___	___	___	paying	___	___	___
storage	___	___	___	nationality	___	___	___
carrying	___	___	___	equipment	___	___	___
employment	___	___	___	insurance	___	___	___
disruptive	___	___	___	fog	___	___	___
dust	___	___	___	destroying	___	___	___
readiness	___	___	___	collision	___	___	___
sharpen	___	___	___	rectangle	___	___	___
humidity	___	___	___	longingly	___	___	___
northward	___	___	___	defensive	___	___	___
buckle	___	___	___	lucky	___	___	___
hedge	___	___	___	laughter	___	___	___
rehearse	___	___	___	spaghetti	___	___	___
shoulder	___	___	___	sailor	___	___	___
mosquito	___	___	___	conscious	___	___	___

RULES

1. A one-syllable word is never divided. **boat**

2. Divide a compound word between the words that make up the compound word. **pan-cake**

3. When a word has a suffix, divide the word between the base word and the suffix. **soft-ness**

4. When a word ends in **le** preceded by a consonant, divide the word before that consonant. When a word ends in **ckle**, divide between the **k** and the **le**. **tur-tle   pick-le**

1. peaches _____

2. handle _____

3. deepen _____

4. pickle _____

5. useful _____

6. mumble _____

7. steering _____

8. headache _____

9. sickness _____

10. handsome _____

11. postage _____

12. knuckle _____

13. blacksmith _____

14. colder _____

15. shackle _____

16. shipment _____

17. purple _____

18. earthquake _____

19. curly _____

20. skyward _____

21. apple _____

22. helpless _____

23. payment _____

24. tickle _____

25. thumbtack _____

26. safest _____

27. shipwreck _____

28. thistle _____

29. angle _____

30. hopscotch _____

31. tumble _____

32. heckle _____

Name _____

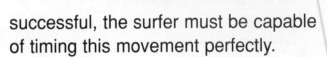

SURFING:
Riding a Wall of Water

The sport of surfing has been practiced for centuries in Hawaii and other Pacific islands. Today, millions of people around the world enjoy the excitement of riding the fastest, tallest waves they can find.

To begin, the surfer, lying flat or kneeling, paddles his board out to the seaward side of the breaking waves. Then he waits patiently for the perfect wave. When he sees the wave he starts paddling toward shore as fast as he can. When the wave reaches the surfer, the board lifts upward and speeds up rapidly. The surfer moves to a standing position and rides down the awesome wall of water, staying just ahead of the breaking crest. To be successful, the surfer must be capable of timing this movement perfectly.

The ride ends when the surfer leans backward to slow the board down and then kicks out over the unbroken wave into the calm waters behind it. An unsuccessful surfer who loses the race against the breaking wave can be "wiped out" (smashed onto the sea floor) by the weight of the collapsing water!

Surfing, like skiing and skateboarding, requires balance, timing, and coordination. What sport do you think is the most exciting? Why?

_____
_____
_____
_____
_____

 **Writing**

You are a reporter for a kids' magazine. Your assignment is to write an article about a surfing competition. Use the helpful hints and the words from the word bank.

Tell where and when.

Tell who won and how.

Tell what happened to the losers.

Describe the surfers' outfits and boards.

Helpful Hints

impressive   enjoyment

successful   direction

happiness   fanciest

colorful   sparkling

endurance   fearless

Name _____

Fill in the circle beside the word that correctly combines each base word and suffix. Write the word on the line.

1. home + ward   _____   ○ homward   ○ homeward

2. wet + est   _____   ○ wettest   ○ wetest

3. simple + ly   _____   ○ simply   ○ simplely

4. precise + sion _____   ○ precisesion   ○ precision

5. act + ive + ly _____   ○ activly   ○ actively

6. universe + ity _____   ○ universsity   ○ university

7. dry + es   _____   ○ dries   ○ dryes

8. marry + age   _____   ○ marryage   ○ marriage

9. fog + y   _____   ○ fogy   ○ foggy

10. value + able   _____   ○ valuable   ○ valueable

▶ Read each sentence. Fill in the circle beside the word that completes the sentence. Write the word on the line.

11. We _____ up the horses for a ride in the desert.
    ○ saddleed   ○ saddled   ○ saddlied

12. A pack horse carried all our _____ .
    ○ baggage   ○ bagage   ○ bagge

13. Our guide checked us out _____ .
    ○ carefuly   ○ carfully   ○ carefully

14. She said that we would _____ make camp at dusk.
    ○ probabley   ○ probablely   ○ probably

15. We headed off in the _____ of the mountains.
    ○ direction   ○ directtion   ○ direcsion

Read the passage. Then answer the questions at the end of the passage.

THE AMERICAN FLAG

The sight of the U.S. flag can be awesome. It is a powerful symbol of our country's greatness. As our country's symbol, the flag must be treated respectfully, never carelessly. Congress has written laws and guidelines for the flag's care and handling.

The flag should always be displayed near the main administration building of every public institution. That includes every school, college, and university. It must be flown at government buildings. The flag should never be displayed lower than other flags. It should be in the center—at the highest point—in a fan-shaped group of flags. When carried, the flag should be held aloft and free.

The flag should never appear on anything temporary or disposable, such as paper napkins, paper plates, or boxes. Its image should not appear on easily soiled items. It should never be used for advertising.

When the flag is raised, lowered, or presented, people in uniform, like soldiers and police officers, should stand at attention and salute. Others should stand facing forward, with their right hands over their hearts.

1. What is the flag a symbol of?

_____

2. How should the U.S. flag be treated?

_____

3. Where should the U.S. flag be displayed?

_____

4. On what items should the flag's image never appear?

_____

5. What should people do when the flag is raised or lowered?

_____

Boo-hoo! Who eight one of my pies?

What do you think it would be like to live here?

Critical Thinking

There are some very unusual things happening in this picture. See how many you can find.

Home Letter

Dear Family,

Over the next several weeks, your child will be learning about vowel combinations that can represent a variety of vowel sounds.

At-Home Activities

▶ With your child, discuss what's wrong in the picture on the other side of this letter. Encourage your child to make a list.

▶ Ask your child to find words in the list that have vowel pairs, such as ai, ay, ea, and ee; digraphs such as oo, ow, aw, and au; and the diphthongs oi and oy. Together, determine how many syllables each word contains.

▶ Go to the library with your child and read about medieval castles. Encourage your child to discuss some of the things he or she discovered.

Book Corner

You and your child might enjoy reading these books together.

Of Swords and Sorcerers
The Adventures of King Arthur and His Knights

by Margaret Hodges and Margery Evernden

The adventures of King Arthur and the Knights of the Round Table come alive in this exciting selection of tales.

Seaward

by Susan Cooper

Two children take off on a magical quest in this fantasy-adventure story.

Sincerely,

Name _____

> **Look at each picture. Find its name in the word bank and write it on the line.**

RULE

In a **vowel pair,** two vowels come together to make one long sound. The first vowel in the pair usually stands for its long sound, and the second is silent.

d**ai**sy

road	train	hay	beads
creature	nails	crow	tie
queen	sheep	toes	cheese

1

_____

2

_____

3

_____

4

_____

5

_____

6

_____

7

_____

8

_____

> **Read each sentence. Complete the sentence with a word from the word bank at the top of the page.**

9. Our class rode a _____ to visit a farm.

10. At the farm we saw brown cows and white _____.

11. We saw a farm worker making _____ in a churn.

12. The farmer made a strange _____ to put in the field.

13. The scarecrow wore a _____ around its neck.

14. Every single _____ flew out of the field because it was scared.

Read the sentences. Underline each word in which you hear the long a sound of the vowel pairs ai and ay. Circle the number of the sentence that describes the picture.

1. Jay wanted to go straight home.

2. He had to wait in line to get a ticket.

3. Jay failed to get on the train.

4. A gray donkey strayed into the daylight.

5. It went straight to the hay.

6. The donkey brayed as it raided the hay.

Read each sentence. Complete the sentence with a word from the word bank.

7. Fay _____ that her room was dreary.

8. The brown walls were too _____.

9. Fay decided to _____ her room.

10. She wanted light _____ walls.

11. She used one _____ of paint.

12. She did one wall a different _____.

13. She put up wallpaper with _____.

14. It _____ outside while Fay painted.

15. She _____ for the paint to dry.

16. She didn't like the _____.

17. Then she hung the pictures on _____.

18. She put yellow curtains on her large _____ window.

bay   gray

rained   waited

plain   delay

paint   way

pail   nails

daisies

complained

Name _____

Say each word in the word bank. Circle the vowel pair in each word that stands for the long **e** sound. Then write each word in the correct column.

| sneeze | meek | leisure | heed | keen | reach |
| seizure | neat | ceiling | peach | seize | reason |

see   **leaf**   **Neil**

_____   _____   _____

_____   _____   _____

_____   _____   _____

_____   _____   _____

Read each sentence. Circle the word that correctly completes the sentence and write it on the line.

1. Peaches are _____ at this time of year.

beaded
reach
cheap

2. Unripened peaches are _____ and hard.

meat
green
keen

3. People sometimes _____ off the fuzzy skin.

flee
lee
peel

4. Eat a juicy peach slowly and at your _____ .

leisure
seizure
ceiling

tried	dried	ties	pried
cries	pliers	fried	pies
lie	supplies	cried	untied

1. People _____ out with joy when the circus arrived.

2. Everyone _____ to see the animals.

3. The workers unloaded the equipment and _____.

4. Meanwhile, the cook _____ chicken for dinner.

5. The baker made _____ for dessert.

6. After dinner, everyone washed and _____ the dishes.

7. Then three clowns wearing striped _____ put on a show.

8. One clown _____ the knot in a rope around a big box.

9. Another clown used _____ to pull out the nails.

10. A third clown popped out when the lid was _____ off.

11. The other two made him _____ down again in the box.

12. Their act brought _____ of laughter from the audience.

> **Would you have enjoyed the clown's performance? Tell why or why not.**

Critical Thinking

Name _____

 Say each word in the word bank. Circle the vowel pair that stands for the long **o** sound. Then write the word in the correct column.

> **RULE**
> The vowel pairs **oa, oe, ow** usually have the long **o** sound.
>
> r**oa**d   t**oe**   bl**ow**

hoe	snow	float	pillow	toe	bowl	poach
boast	doe	row	throat	soap	woe	bow

foe

coat

Joe

crow

_____   _____   _____

_____   _____   _____

_____   _____   _____

_____   _____   _____

_____   _____   _____

Read each definition. Choose a word from the word bank at the top of the page that matches the definition and write it on the line.

1. one way to move a boat _____

2. something soft for your head _____

3. a garden tool _____

4. a hair ribbon _____

5. one way to cook eggs _____

6. sadness _____

7. used when you swallow _____

8. what you eat cereal from _____

9. something to wash with _____

Word Bank:
tomorrow
pleased
speak
seeds
main
due
row
straight
eat
goat
peek
hoe
boasting
keep
continue
narrow
receive
need

1. A gardener will _____ to the class.

2. Then _____ we will plant vegetables.

3. He will _____ to give us help when we need it.

4. A report about gardening will be _____ next week.

5. It will _____ to include the following rules.

6. First buy _____ to plant in the garden.

7. Use a _____ to dig up the dirt.

8. Complete one _____ before starting another.

9. The rows should be _____, not wide.

10. The rows should also be _____, not crooked.

11. The _____ thing is to water the seeds.

12. Seeds will grow if they _____ water and get sun.

13. Soon, little plants will _____ out of the soil.

14. You will be _____ to everyone about your garden.

15. Do not let a _____ get into the garden.

16. It will _____ all your plants.

17. You will not be _____ if that happens.

18. Build a fence to _____ animals out.

What do you think are the three most important rules for planting and caring for a garden?

Critical Thinking

Seeds

Name _____

Say the name of each picture. Circle the picture if you hear the short sound of **e** in its name.

RULE

In a **vowel digraph,** two vowels together can make a long or short sound, or have a special sound all their own. The vowel digraph **ea** can stand for the short **e** sound.

st**ea**dy

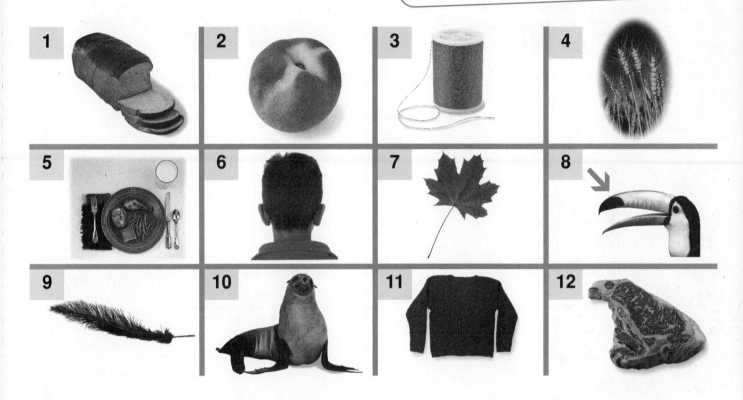

Read each sentence. Complete the sentence with a word from the word bank.

13. The _____ was windy and cool.

14. Beth got _____ to go outside.

15. A walk would make her feel _____ .

16. Beth put a hat on her _____ .

17. She took out her _____ gloves.

18. Her favorite _____ had a hole in it.

19. Beth needed _____ to mend it.

20. She used the needle with a _____ hand.

sweater	ready
weather	healthy
thread	head
steady	leather

RULE

The vowel digraphs **ei** and **ey** can stand for the long **a** sound.

w**ei**gh   ob**ey**

eight	obey	sleigh	hey	reindeer
neighbor	veil	prey	survey	convey

reins

_____

_____

_____

_____

they

_____

_____

_____

_____

Read the sentences and questions below. Answer each question with a response from the word bank.

watching and observing   rules

transmitted or sent out

1. The **reign** of King Henry lasted for many years. If a king **reigns,** what does he do?

_____

2. King Henry had royal guards keep his advisors under **surveillance.** What would the royal guards be doing to keep the advisors under **surveillance?**

_____

3. The royal guards **conveyed** the king's wishes and orders to the people. What does **conveyed** mean?

_____

Name _____

Read each pair of sentences. Then underline each word in which ie stands for the long e sound. Circle the number of the sentence that describes the picture.

RULE
The vowel digraph **ie** can stand for the long **e** sound.
p**ie**ce

1. The army marched across the field.

2. The castle was under siege by an army.

3. The chief lifted up his shield.

4. The battle stopped for a brief moment.

5. Everyone believed that the castle was lost.

6. A piece of stone fell off the wall.

Read each sentence. Circle the word that correctly completes the sentence and write it on the line.

7. "Please hand me that _____ of blue cloth," said Aunt Betsy.
        achieve   siege   piece

8. Her _____, Lucy, gave her the cloth.
        piece   niece   wield

9. "The flag will have thirteen stars on a _____ of blue," Betsy told Lucy.
        yield   field   shield

10. "It will be the _____ symbol of our new nation," she said.
        chief   grief   thief

Read each definition. Write the word from the word bank that matches the definition. Put a check (√) beside the answer if the letters **ie** stand for the long **e** sound.

grief	chief	field	mantelpiece
relieved	fielder	piece	shield
shriek	dried	die	belief
fried	brief	pierce	thief

1. a place where corn and wheat grow _____

2. another word for **faith** _____

3. a portion of something can also be called this _____

4. a loud, shrill sound _____

5. eggs can be cooked this way _____

6. the way you feel when news is good _____

7. head person in the fire department _____

8. what flowers do without water _____

9. no longer wet or damp _____

10. shelf on a fireplace _____

11. a word that describes something short _____

12. person on a baseball team _____

13. deep sorrow _____

14. a police officer's badge _____

15. to make a hole through something _____

16. a person who steals _____

Lesson 44
Vowel digraph ie

Name _____

Say the name of each picture. Circle the picture if its name has the same vowel sound you hear in **too** and **moon**.

> **RULE**
> One sound the vowel digraph **oo** can stand for is the vowel sound you hear in **too** and **moon**.

1

2

3

4

5

6

7

8

9

10

11

12

Read each sentence. Complete the sentence with a word from the word bank.

13. An owl sat silently in the _____.

14. A _____ of light fell on a small rabbit.

15. Suddenly, the owl _____ off the branch.

16. Her flight was _____ and silent.

17. She made a quick _____ and dove down.

18. The owl let out a soft _____ of pride.

19. She would not let her catch get _____.

20. She carried the _____ to her waiting owlets.

hoot
zoom
loop
loose
smooth
pool
moonlight
food
proof
swooped

Lesson 45
Vowel digraph oo

99

Read the word in each box. Then draw a picture that shows what the word means.

1	2	3
book	football	foot

4	5	6
hood	woods	hook

Read each sentence. Complete the sentence with a word from the word bank.

notebook	looked
barefoot	shook
crook	brook
hook	stood

7. The detective hung her coat on the

_____ by the door.

8. She sat down to check the notes in her

_____ .

9. She _____ her head in anger.

10. The _____ she was after had escaped.

11. The detective _____ up and walked to the window.

12. She _____ down at the dark, empty street.

Read the words in the word bank. Then write each word in the correct column.

RULE

The vowel digraph **oo** can stand for the vowel sound you hear in **too** or the vowel sound you hear in **look**.

too   **look**

_____   _____

_____   _____

_____   _____

_____   _____

_____   _____

bloom	cool	troop	stood	cook	shook
soot	spoon	wood	foot	roost	noon

Read each sentence. Circle each word in which **oo** stands for the vowel sound you hear in **too**. Underline each word in which **oo** stands for the sound you hear in **look**.

1. It was a cool night with a full moon.

2. The little crook was looking for food.

3. It scooted into the yard and shook the cans.

4. The campers in the wooden cabin were spooked.

5. They stood quietly in the small room.

6. Then the cook grabbed a broom.

7. The campers looked out into the moonlit night.

8. They felt like fools when they took in the sight.

9. Their crook was a raccoon.

Lesson 46
Vowel digraph oo

101

A Walk in the Woods

As you read look for clues that tell you what time of year the story takes place.

Critical Thinking

Leslie and Carrie Underwood put on their boots and took a moonlit walk after the heavy rainfall. The blooming flowers in the yard drooped from the rain. The kids set out down the footpath and into the woods. Along the path, the moonlight shined on mushrooms and toadstools. A raccoon snooped around the dogwood trees. Leslie and Carrie crossed a brook and passed the house of a woodcutter. They came out of the woods on the other side of a grove of cottonwood trees.

Soon the kids came to the smooth sandy shore of a lagoon. Many little creatures lived there in nooks and holes. Nearby they took a look at an insect emerging from its cocoon. A coot or a loon, they were not sure which, swooped down on the deck of a sloop anchored in the lagoon.

It began to grow cool, so Leslie and Carrie trooped back home. Suddenly Carrie let out a whoop. Something wet and furry had scooted past her. They guessed it was a woodchuck who had been looking for food. After a good snack, Leslie and Carrie soon called it a day.

1. What word tells you it was nighttime? _____

2. What snooped around the dogwoods? _____

3. What body of water did the girls come upon? _____

4. What kind of boat was anchored there? _____

5. Name two birds you read about. _____

Name _____

Say the name of each picture. Then circle its name.

1 	autumn laundry naughty	2 	draw dawn thaw

3  raw / thaw / paw

4	fault saucer faucet	5	claws jaws laws

6 sausages / saucer / applesauce

Read each sentence. Complete the sentence with a word from the word bank.

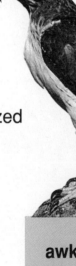

7. It was _____ , and the leaves had changed colors.

8. The large bird _____ and waited for the right moment.

9. Then the _____ swooped down and seized its prey.

10. It had _____ its dinner.

11. The hawk is not _____ but very graceful in flight.

12. Its _____ are sharp and powerful.

13. It is a patient and _____ hunter.

14. The hawk _____ the food back to its nest.

15. The baby hawks greeted it with _____ .

awkward	squawks
author	autumn
claws	hawk
hauled	caught
cautious	paused

Read each sentence and find the picture that goes with it. Write the number of the sentence on the line under the picture. Then circle the words in the sentence that have the aw sound.

1. A jaunty dinosaur draws a picture.

2. The saucy leprechaun does a somersault.

3. The haunted house looks gaudy.

4. A haughty fawn is sprawled on the ice.

5. The scrawny cat slept in a drawer.

6. The paunchy clown sat on the lawn and bawled.

7. A straw was caught in the faucet.

8. The cautious puppy gnawed a bone.

_____

_____

_____

_____

_____

_____

_____

_____

Name _____

THE GREAT AND SMALL OF DINOSAURS

If you believe that all dinosaurs were huge, meat-eating creatures, you are wrong. The smallest dinosaur yet found, Compsognathus, was the size of a large chicken. It measured two feet in length and weighed about 6.6 pounds. Its name means "pretty jaw"! Compsognathus walked on two legs and caught its food—bugs and lizards—with its small, clawed front paws.

Another small dinosaur, the three-foot-long *Lesothosaurus*, lived on plants. *Lesothosaurus* had flat, leaf-shaped teeth and a hooked beak.

The largest dinosaurs—nicknamed "supersaurs" by the scientists who discovered them—were plant eaters, too. They had very small brains and moved slowly. Scientists estimate that they measured 50 feet in height. That's tall enough to look into the windows of a five-story building!

However, even this giant was dwarfed by a dinosaur whose remains have been found in New Mexico. The earth probably shook when the awesome *Seismosaurus* roamed the land. The *Seismosaurus* surveyed the land from a height of more than 130 feet. If you ever saw *Seismosaurus*, you would know why scientists named it "earth shaker"!

Which of the dinosaurs mentioned in the passage would you like to learn more about? Why?

_____

_____

_____

_____

Writing

Suppose you are a time-traveling reporter. Journey back to the time when seismosaurs shook the earth to take a first-hand look at these awesome beasts. Write a description of your observations. Use words from the word bank.

awful	haunches	brawny
cause	assault	survey
believed	proof	stood

Helpful Hints

Describe where the dinosaurs lived, what they looked like, how they acted, and how you felt when you first saw them.

Name _____

Look at each picture. Find its name in the word bank and write it on the line.

boil   noise   coins
royalty
soil   boy   cowboy

DEFINITION

A **diphthong** is made up of two vowels sounded so that both vowels blend together as one sound. The diphthongs **oi** and **oy** stand for the same sound.

c**oi**n   b**oy**

1
_____

2
_____

3
_____

4
_____

5
_____

6
_____

Read each word. Find its definition in the second column. Write the letter of the definition on the line beside the word.

7. loyal _____   **A.** slightly damp

8. embroider _____   **B.** light bluish-green color

9. voyage _____   **C.** make a design on cloth with needle and thread

10. moist _____   **D.** faithful

11. broil _____   **E.** a long trip to a place far away

12. poison _____   **F.** something that can cause death

13. annoy _____   **G.** bother or pester

14. turquoise _____ **H.** a way to cook something

© MCP All rights reserved. Copying strictly prohibited.

Lesson 49
Diphthongs oi, oy

107

POP!

Oil sizzles in the pan. Pour in corn kernels. Put the lid on tightly to avoid being hit by flying kernels. Then listen for the first noise. Pop! After that first joyful pop, all the kernels seem poised to explode at once. The noisy pops come rapidly. When the noise stops, it's safe to remove the lid. Then enjoy your first taste of popcorn. You'll never be disappointed. Yum!

What makes popcorn pop? It's the moisture inside the hard kernel. When popcorn is heated, the moisture in it boils and forms steam. The steam makes the kernel explode and pop.

You can boil corn in water. You can broil it on a grill. But every boy and girl's favorite choice is popping it. Did you know that scientists found popcorn more than 5,000 years old in a cave? (Do you think it was too spoiled to eat?) Some Native Americans used popcorn, instead of coins, for money. Others enjoyed wearing it as jewelry. At the first Thanksgiving, in 1621, Native Americans brought popcorn to the feast for the Pilgrims' enjoyment!

1. Which word tells how popping corn sounds?

_____

2. Why should you cover the pan tightly?

_____

3. Name three ways popcorn can be cooked.

_____

4. What causes popcorn to pop?

_____

What fact about popcorn did you find the most interesting?

Critical Thinking

Read each pair of sentences. Then underline each word in which **ew** stands for the sound you hear in **new.** Circle the number of the sentence that describes the picture.

RULE

The diphthong **ew** stands for the vowel sound you hear in **new.** This is almost the same sound you hear in **moon.**

1. The spaceship flew through space on its long journey.

2. The stars were like jewels in the dark of space.

3. The crew exercised a few hours every day.

4. Earth grew smaller in the view screen.

5. They knew their story would be in all the newspapers.

6. The crew set foot on new ground.

Read each sentence. Complete the sentence with a word from the word bank.

7. The _____ pitcher eyed the batter closely.

8. He _____ he had to strike out the batter to win the game.

9. The pitcher _____ back his arm and let the ball fly.

10. Crack! The runner _____ around the bases.

11. The outfielder _____ the ball to home too late.

12. The final score would be on the late _____.

drew   blew
news   strewn
threw   knew
shrewd
flew

1. loyal
2. Joyce
3. jewel
4. noisy
5. annoy
6. chew
7. spoiled
8. soil
9. nephew
10. poison
11. employ
12. threw
13. destroy
14. coin
15. stew
16. point
17. oil
18. royal
19. dew
20. moist
21. newspaper
22. screws
23. avoid
24. flew

Read each sentence. Think about the way the first two words in boldface are related. Then choose one of the words from above to complete the analogy.

DEFINITION

An **analogy** compares different things. Analogies show how pairs of things are alike.

A **car** is to a **road** as a **boat** is to **water.**

25. **Hammer** is to **nails** as **screwdriver** is to _____.

26. **Vegetables** are to **salad** as **meat** is to _____.

27. **Desert** is to **dry** as **swamp** is to _____.

28. **Niece** is to **girl** as _____ is to **boy.**

29. **Dollar** is to **bill** as **quarter** is to _____.

30. **Milk** is to **sip** as **apple** is to _____.

31. **Dismiss** is to **fire** as **hire** is to _____.

32. **Radio** is to **listen** as _____ is to **read.**

33. **Hay** is to **horse** as _____ is to **machine.**

34. **Fresh** is to **food** as _____ is to **garbage.**

35. **Whisper** is to **quiet** as **shout** is to _____.

36. **Run** is to **ran** as **throw** is to _____.

37. **Build** is to **create** as **demolish** is to _____.

38. **Tip** is to **brush** as _____ is to **pencil.**

39. **See** is to **saw** as **fly** is to _____.

40. **Ice** is to **frost** as **water** is to _____.

Name _____

RULE

The diphthongs **ou** and **ow** often stand for the vowel sound you hear in **loud** and **down.**

1 claw clown

2 bless blouse

3 1,000 thousand thaw

4 shower shout

5 floors flowers

6 cloud clog

▶ **Read the sentences and questions below. Answer each question with a response from the word bank. Write it on the line.**

7. The crew on the boat was **rowdy** and had to be quieted down. What does **rowdy** mean?

_____

8. The crew was on a **scow** that was hauling garbage down the river. What is a **scow?**

_____

9. The crew was **doused** when a sudden rainstorm came up. What does **doused** mean?

_____

10. The captain **scowled** at the bad behavior of the crew. What did the captain do if he **scowled?**

_____

a boat used to haul cargo

drenched

disorderly and rough

looked angry

Lesson 51
Diphthongs ou, ow

111

1. There wasn't a _____ in the sky.

2. We were going to climb the _____.

3. Grandpa said he would _____ for a campsite.

4. We were _____ to bring a few things.

5. We would sleep on the _____.

6. That night we heard a very _____ sound.

7. We all thought that it was a wolf _____.

8. The next morning we went _____ the mountain.

down

howling

cloud

loud

mountain

scout

allowed

ground

9. There was a celebration in the _____.

10. A large _____ of people gathered.

11. They were _____ and noisy.

12. The town _____ was dedicating the fountain.

13. The mayor _____, "one, two, three!"

14. Water spurted from the _____.

15. The crowd _____ loudly and clapped.

16. The people were _____ of their town.

fountain

proud

council

town

counted

shouted

crowd

rowdy

Name _____

1. Do you know that tomorrow is the party?

2. No one will be allowed in without a costume.

3. I will be a clown wearing a big bow.

4. Ted is going to show up as a flower in a bowl.

5. Kim is going to be a brown owl.

6. She will borrow a pillow to stuff in her costume.

7. Dad said we should be mellow, not rowdy.

8. Anyhow, the band will drown out our noise.

ow as in cow	ow as in snow
_____	_____
_____	_____
_____	_____
_____	_____
_____	_____
_____	_____

1. The frowning clown was employed to make the crowd of thousands howl with joy.

2. The shrewd cowboy pounced on the steer while avoiding the points of his long horns.

3. The noisy nephew annoyed his aunt when he pointed and shouted at the flower show.

4. The powerful family threw coins from a tower into a fountain.

Name _____

Say each word. Write its pair of vowels on the first line.
Then write the number of syllables you hear
in the word on the second line.

When you listen for the number of
syllables in a word, remember that a
vowel pair or a diphthong stands for
one vowel sound.

g**oa**t   **oi**ntment

	Pair of Vowels	Number of Syllables		Pair of Vowels	Number of Syllables
1. spoonful	oo	2	19. loyal	o	2
2. noisy	oi	2	20. double	ou	2
3. repeat	ea	2	21. moisten	oi	2
4. thought	ou	2	22. appear	ea	2
5. haunted	ou	2	23. breakfast	ea	2
6. wealthy	ea	2	24. piece	ie	1
7. instead	ea	2	25. ounce	ou	1
8. receive	ei	2	26. because	ou	2
9. jewelry	o	3	27. straight	ai	1
10. awkward	o	2	28. pillow	o	2
11. lied	ie	1	29. soup	ou	1
12. chief	ie	1	30. eighty	ei	2
13. moonlight	oo	2	31. touch	ou	1
14. house	ou	1	32. soul	ou	1
15. avenue	ue	3	33. laundry	au	2
16. withdraw	o	2	34. annoy	o	2
17. flow	o	1	35. true	ue	1
18. dainty	ai	2	36. blooming	oo	2

Underline the pair of vowels in the words. If the two vowels stand for one sound, write 1 on the first line. If the two vowels are sounded separately, write 2 on the first line. Then divide the words into syllables using hyphens, and write them on the second line.

When two vowels stand for one vowel sound, do not divide the word between the two vowels.

por-tr**ai**t   r**ea**-son

When two vowels are sounded separately, divide the word between the two vowels.

ra-d**i-o**   cr**u-e**l

	Vowel Sounds	Syllables		Vowel Sounds	Syllables
poison	___	_____	dialect	___	_____
diagnose	___	_____	couch	___	_____
dinosaur	___	_____	create	___	_____
area	___	_____	quiet	___	_____
saucer	___	_____	tower	___	_____
diary	___	_____	thousand	___	_____
casual	___	_____	ideas	___	_____
season	___	_____	screw	___	_____
raccoons	___	_____	loudest	___	_____
riot	___	_____	defiant	___	_____
survey	___	_____	royalty	___	_____
situate	___	_____	realize	___	_____
pheasant	___	_____	shriek	___	_____
cereal	___	_____	headline	___	_____
really	___	_____	diesel	___	_____

Lesson 53
Syllables in words with two vowels

Name _____

How to Make a SNOW GLOBE

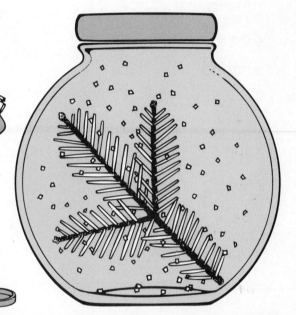

You could buy a new snow globe at a store for a few coins. Or you can make one of your own that can't be found in any store. Here's how.

Materials

a clear, round glass jar with screw-on lid

aluminum foil

one or more toy figures or a piece of an evergreen branch

water

liquid dish detergent

1. Wash out the jar and remove any labels.
2. Make "snow" by cutting a piece of aluminum foil into very, very tiny pieces. The best way to do this is first to cut thin strips along one edge of the foil. Then cut off the strips into tiny pieces. The smaller the pieces, the more real the "snow" will look.
3. Put the foil flakes and the toy figures or branch in the jar.

4. Fill the jar to the top with water. Add just one drop of detergent. The detergent will keep the foil snowflakes from floating. Tightly screw on the lid.
5. Now make a winter snowstorm by turning the snow globe upside down. Give it a gentle shake and then set it down right-side up. Let it snow and enjoy the storm!

Why don't you want the snowflakes to float?

_____
_____
_____
_____

Could you teach someone how to do an art project, play a game, or make a toy? Write a set of directions for how to make or do something. Use words from the word bank.

around

moisten

newspaper

down

employ

screw

found

few

join

powerful

_____

_____

_____

_____

_____

_____

_____

_____

_____

_____

_____

_____

_____

_____

_____

_____

_____

_____

List materials at the beginning.
Think about each step you do.
Write the steps in order.
Use numbers or words such as first, then, and next.

Helpful Hints

Name _____

 Read each sentence. Fill in the circle beside the word that correctly completes the sentence. Write the word on the line.

1. Naturalists _____ how well animals perform.   ○ measure   ○ mayor

2. They have _____ out many new facts.   ○ field   ○ found

3. Here are some fun facts you may not have _____.   ○ knight   ○ known

4. A Goliath beetle can lift 850 times its own _____.   ○ weather   ○ weight

5. To do that, you'd have to pick up four _____ buses!   ○ school   ○ scoot

6. When hunting its _____ of birds, the peregrine falcon dives at over 100 miles per hour!   ○ prey   ○ gray

7. It _____ a bird in its strong talons.   ○ deceives   ○ seizes

8. The basilisk lizard has fringed _____ on its feet.   ○ trout   ○ toes

9. These let it run at high _____ across water!   ○ speed   ○ green

10. A dolphin's skin has a lot of _____ in it.   ○ bowls   ○ oil

11. This helps it _____ great speeds.   ○ achieve   ○ believe

12. Emperor penguins can _____ underwater 18 minutes!   ○ remain   ○ decay

13. Some birds can _____ to amazing heights.   ○ store   ○ soar

14. A vulture _____ hitting an airplane at 36,900 feet!   ○ hid   ○ died

15. _____ do you think it could breathe up there?   ○ Out   ○ How

Read the story and answer the questions.

MAYA LIN, MEMORIAL MAKER

When the Vietnam Veterans Memorial in Washington, D.C., was first built, it caused a lot of talk. It was a new idea for a memorial—just two walls cut into the earth, with the names of those who died in the war. Angry crowds tried to keep the memorial from being built. But the government went ahead, and it was dedicated on Veterans Day 1982.

People were awed by the "Wall." Many cried as they stood before it reading the soldiers' names. Everyone agreed that the memorial had power to cause deep feelings. Now thousands of visitors are drawn to it each year.

Architect Maya Lin was just 21 years old and a Yale University student when she drew up plans for the memorial. Her design beat out those of 1,420 people who entered the contest to design the memorial. Because her work is so good, Lin keeps very busy. She enjoys what she does and is always ready to begin a new project.

1. Why did the Vietnam Veterans Memorial cause a lot of talk?

_____

2. How did people react to the completed memorial?

_____

3. What did people agree about the Wall?

_____

4. What did Maya Lin have to do to win the contest to design the memorial?

_____

5. How does Lin feel about her work?

_____

AT A ZANY ZOO

Let's slide down the giraffe's neck
And blow the rhinos' horns.
But don't let the ostriches peck
And don't step on the hippo's corns.

We'll pay the pelicans' bills
With cash from the kangaroo's pouch.
We won't pluck the porcupines' quills.
If we did, you'd hear us yell "Ouch!"

Let's sail on a whale for a while,
Then unpack the elephants' trunks.
But beware of the crocodile's smile
And don't get too close to the skunks.

What does the word zany mean? Why do you think the poem is called "At a Zany Zoo"?

Critical Thinking

Home Letter

Dear Family,

In the next few weeks we will be learning how to make words plural, how to add apostrophes to show possession, and how to combine words into contractions.

At-Home Activities

▶ Read the poem on the other side of this letter with your child. Talk about what each contraction in the poem stands for. With your child, point out plural words and words that show possession.

▶ Talk about the words in the poem that have two meanings (horns, bills, trunks). Then, together, see if you can create funny new lines about other animals to add to the poem.

▶ With your child, look for contractions in other printed material such as newspapers and magazines. Ask your child to tell what each contraction stands for.

Book Corner

You and your child might enjoy reading these books together. Look for them in your local library.

Morgan's Zoo

by James Howe
Discover how twins team up with a zookeeper to protect a neighborhood zoo in this beautifully illustrated story.

Bunnicula

by Deborah and James Howe

When an abandoned rabbit joins the family, Chester the cat and Howard the dog become suspicious. They think it's more than a coincidence that the rabbit is named after the vampire Dracula.

Sincerely,

Name _____

Read each word and write its plural form on the line.

1. tax _____

2. buzz _____

3. branch _____

4. waltz _____

5. glass _____

6. fox _____

7. wish _____

8. patch _____

Read each sentence. Underline the word in the sentence that has the suffix es. Write its base word on the line.

9. The forecaster puts on her glasses. _____

10. She watches the weather reports coming in. _____

11. Ten more inches of snow fell last night. _____

12. The mountain passes are closed due to snow. _____

13. There are patches of ice on every road. _____

14. The snow has caused branches to fall across roads. _____

15. Crews use axes to chop and remove the limbs. _____

16. The forecaster has two wishes. _____

17. She wants bright sunshine and warm sandy beaches. _____

Read each word. Write its plural form on the line.

1. fly _____

2. mystery _____

3. tray _____

4. beauty _____

5. hobby _____

6. medley _____

7. melody _____

8. injury _____

Read each sentence. Complete the sentence with the plural form of the word at the right.

9. It is fun to explore the _____ near your home.   (library)

10. Which _____ do you enjoy reading?   (story)

11. I enjoy reading _____.   (mystery)

12. I also like books about _____.   (spy)

13. Some children like books about _____.   (cowboy)

14. Some people like to read about sports _____.   (victory)

15. My sister likes to read about lawyers and _____.   (jury)

16. My dad studies books about _____.   (hobby)

17. My mom reads about how to make _____.   (pastry)

18. Do you enjoy books about other _____?   (country)

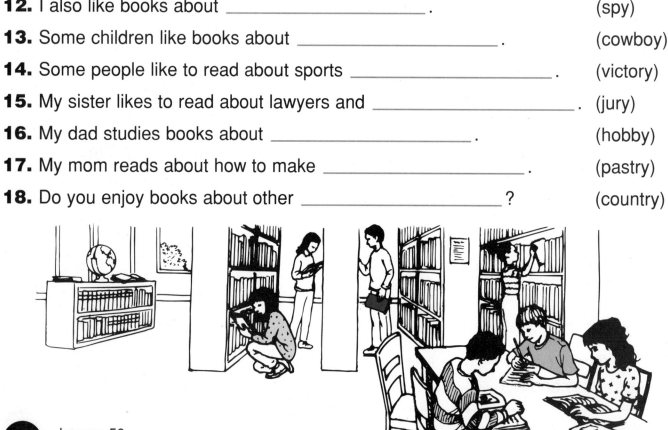

Name _____

Read each word and write its plural form on the line.

1. half _____

2. thief _____

3. life _____   7. loaf _____

4. shelf _____   8. elf _____

5. knife _____   9. self _____

6. calf _____   10. leaf _____

Read each sentence. Write a word from the word bank to complete the sentence. Then write its base word on the line.

shelves

hooves

wolves

thieves

lives

loaves

calves

wives

themselves

11. Farmers of long ago led very

busy _____ .   _____

12. They rose early to tend their cows

and _____ .   _____

13. They made horseshoes for their

horses' _____ .   _____

14. They put up fences to keep out

animals such as _____ .   _____

15. The fox and the wolf were _____   _____

that stole the farmers' chickens.

16. The farmers' _____ worked very hard, too.   _____

17. They filled the _____ with jars of   _____

vegetables and homemade jam.

Read each word and write its plural form on the line. Then read each sentence below and choose either the singular or plural form of a word to complete the sentence. If you are unsure of the spelling of a word, look it up in your dictionary.

1. kangaroo _____

2. rodeo _____

3. banjo _____

4. lasso _____

5. solo _____

6. sombrero _____

7. soprano _____

8. bronco _____

9. hero _____

10. photo _____

11. igloo _____

12. patio _____

13. In a _____ cowhands do all sorts of tricks.

14. A singer sings a _____ to open the show.

15. Some cowhands play tunes on _____.

16. Cowhands ride bucking _____.

17. These horses jump up and down like _____.

18. Cowhands use their _____ to rope calves.

19. Some riders wear large _____ on their heads.

20. Rodeo stars can be real _____ to children.

Name _____

► **Write each plural form beside the correct singular form.**

1. man _____

2. foot _____

3. ox _____

4. woman _____

5. mouse _____

6. child _____

7. goose _____

8. tooth _____

oxen	mice
feet	children
mice	men
children	geese
women	teeth

► **Read each sentence. Write the plural form of the word in parentheses to complete the sentence.**

9. The _____ were learning about animals in school. (child)

10. They learned that baby _____ are born without fur. (mouse)

11. _____ swim far up rivers to lay their eggs. (Salmon)

12. Sharks have many rows of sharp _____. (tooth)

13. _____ lose their antlers in winter and grow new ones in spring. (Deer)

14. The antlers of _____ can spread six feet or more. (moose)

15. Moles have large _____ that they use as shovels. (foot)

16. Most Canada _____ fly south for the winter. (goose)

Across

2. potato
4. child
5. moose
6. fly
11. ox
12. knife
15. trout
16. leaf
17. mouse
19. kangaroo
21. waltz
22. tooth

Down

1. woman
2. patio
3. shelf
5. melody
7. loaf
8. elk
9. foot
10. inch
13. story
14. wolf
18. fox
20. goose

Name _____

▶ **Read each sentence. Circle the word that correctly completes the sentence, and write it on the line.**

RULE

The possessive form of a word is used to show that a person or animal owns, has, or possesses something. To make a singular noun show possession, add an apostrophe and an **s** (**'s**) at the end of the word.

Joan**'s** skirt   the baby**'s** bottle

the horse**'s** tail

1. Gerbils are the _____ favorite pets.   classes   class's

2. The _____ favorite is the hamster.   teachers   teacher's

3. The _____ fur is thick and soft.   hamsters   hamster's

4. _____ have fur that is fuzzy.   Gerbils   Gerbil's

5. The _____ active time can be day or night.   animals   animals'

6. Their _____ are made of glass.   cages   cage's

7. They spend hours on their _____.   wheels   wheel's

▶ **Read each word and write its possessive form on the line.**

8. boy _____   **9.** Leslie _____

10. nurse _____   **11.** dancer _____

12. girl _____   **13.** man _____

14. chicken _____   **15.** dentist _____

16. friend _____   **17.** month _____

Read each group of words. If the words show that more than one person or thing has something, write **more than one** on the line. If the words show that only one person or thing has something, write **one**.

1. the lumberjack's coat _____

2. the chefs' convention _____

3. the kangaroo's ears _____

4. the woman's hand _____

5. the mothers' march _____

6. the ladies' coats _____

7. the fish's fins _____

8. the clowns' act _____

9. the hero's welcome _____

10. the boys' bikes _____

11. the babies' bibs _____

12. the general's office _____

13. the pianists' contest _____

14. the giraffe's neck _____

15. the orioles' songs _____

16. the hunters' caps _____

17. the puppy's toy _____

18. the wolves' den _____

Name _____

| giraffe's | class's | porcupines' | judges' | eels' | world's |
| bear's | squids' | teacher's | | ostrich's | birds' | dolphins' |

1. The _____ science reports are due today.

2. One _____ class has entered a contest.

3. The _____ long neck makes it the tallest animal.

4. The _____ largest desert is the Sahara.

5. A _____ heart beat slows when hibernating.

6. The _____ long bodies make them look like snakes.

7. The _____ large body and small wings keep it from flying.

8. Some _____ nests look like hanging baskets.

9. The _____ tentacles are used to catch prey.

10. The _____ blowholes enable them to breathe.

11. The _____ quills measure up to five inches long.

12. The _____ decisions on the winners will be final.

 Write the words from the word bank at the top of the page in the correct columns.

Singular Possessives

_____

_____

_____

_____

_____

_____

Plural Possessives

_____

_____

_____

_____

_____

_____

Read the sentence in each box and draw a picture to show what the sentence means. Then circle the word or words that show possession.

1. The pretty princess drives her neighbor's sleigh.

2. Ed's shirt and the girls' blouses are the color turquoise.

3. Two persons' crimson cloaks and someone's feathered hat hung in the closet.

4. The girls' heads were adorned with wreaths made from flower petals and birds' feathers.

In the first column, write the two words the contraction stands for. In the second column, write the letter or letters left out of the contraction.

RULE

A **contraction** is a short way of writing two words. The two words are written together, but one or more letters are left out. An **apostrophe** stands for the missing letters.

I am = **I'm**   it is = **it's**

can not = **can't**

Words   **Letter or Letters Left Out**

1. haven't _____   _____

2. isn't _____   _____

3. we've _____   _____

4. you're _____   _____

5. they'll _____   _____

6. let's _____   _____

7. didn't _____   _____

8. I've _____   _____

Underline the contraction in each sentence. Then write the two words it stands for on the line.

9. We're reading a book about beavers.   _____

10. We haven't read about beavers before.   _____

11. They're very interesting animals.   _____

12. A beaver's tail isn't useless.   _____

13. It's shaped like a canoe paddle.   _____

14. They'll slap their tails to warn others of danger.   _____

1. can not _____
2. I am _____
3. was not _____
4. he will _____
5. will not _____
6. you will _____
7. could not _____
8. it is _____
9. do not _____
10. are not _____
11. they have _____
12. where is _____
13. that is _____
14. we are _____
15. I will _____
16. she is _____
17. were not _____
18. should not _____

Read each sentence. Underline the words that can form a contraction.
Write the contraction on the line beside the sentence.

19. What is a cloud? _____

20. Let us think about clouds. _____

21. Clouds are not marshmallows or cotton. _____

22. They are drops of water. _____

23. That is a fact. _____

24. It is hard to believe this about clouds. _____

25. Clouds will not always bring rain. _____

26. They will sometimes bring snow or sleet. _____

27. A cloud can not move without wind. _____

28. I have learned a little about clouds. _____

Name _____

Say each word. Write the number of vowels you see in each word on the first line. Then write the number of vowels you hear in each word on the second line.

	Vowels				Vowels	
	See	**Hear**			**See**	**Hear**
1. bushes	_____	_____	**18.** surveys		_____	_____
2. mysteries	_____	_____	**19.** halves		_____	_____
3. heroes	_____	_____	**20.** beliefs		_____	_____
4. glasses	_____	_____	**21.** teeth		_____	_____
5. tomatoes	_____	_____	**22.** waltzes		_____	_____
6. thieves	_____	_____	**23.** pianos		_____	_____
7. daughters	_____	_____	**24** melodies		_____	_____
8. foxes	_____	_____	**25.** solos		_____	_____
9. geese	_____	_____	**26.** potatoes		_____	_____
10. injuries	_____	_____	**27.** boxes		_____	_____
11. sombreros	_____	_____	**28.** clowns		_____	_____
12. guesses	_____	_____	**29.** leaves		_____	_____
13. sopranos	_____	_____	**30.** activities		_____	_____
14. shelves	_____	_____	**31.** buzzes		_____	_____
15. cookies	_____	_____	**32.** lassos		_____	_____
16. wives	_____	_____	**33.** elves		_____	_____
17. scratches	_____	_____	**34.** patches		_____	_____

Study the following rules. Then read the words below. On the first line after each word, write the number of the rule that is used to divide the word into syllables. On the second line, use hyphens to divide the word into syllables.

1. circus _____ _____

2. odor _____ _____

3. carton _____ _____

4. habit _____ _____

5. label _____ _____

6. modern _____ _____

7. plenty _____ _____

8. silent _____ _____

9. olive _____ _____

10. tender _____ _____

11. legal _____ _____

12. donate _____ _____

13. punish _____ _____

14. tarnish _____ _____

15. vacant _____ _____

16. medal _____ _____

17. photo _____ _____

18. velvet _____ _____

19. frozen _____ _____

20. lizard _____ _____

21. publish _____ _____

22. radish _____ _____

23. petal _____ _____

24. lantern _____ _____

25. picture _____ _____

26. robin _____ _____

27. tiger _____ _____

28. famous _____ _____

Name _____

Morse Code to Be Replaced

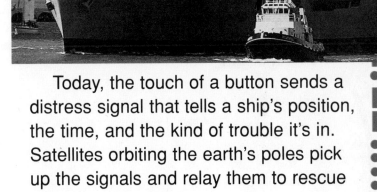

In 1999 the last official message in Morse code will be sent over the airways. Modern technology has outgrown Samuel Morse's system of using dots and dashes to stand for letters of the alphabet.

Long ago, before radios were invented, ships' crews used flags, lanterns, and foghorns to call for help. This system only worked if the ships were near each other. Then Guglielmo Marconi invented the wireless telegraph. Using Morse's code of dots and dashes, ships could tap out messages to each other. This greatly improved safety at sea since ships didn't have to be close to each other to call for help.

Today, the touch of a button sends a distress signal that tells a ship's position, the time, and the kind of trouble it's in. Satellites orbiting the earth's poles pick up the signals and relay them to rescue stations' receivers.

By 1999 all ships must have special radio beacons. If a ship sinks, the beacon will float free and continue to send out distress signals. This system has already saved the lives of more than 1,000 men, women, and children.

How do you think a ship's captain of the past would react if he were brought to the present and shown this new survival technology? Give reasons for your opinion.

_____

_____

_____

_____

_____

_____

_____

 **Writing**

Write a message to a friend in the space below. Then encode your message in Morse code. Exchange messages with a friend and decode the message you receive. Use the words from the word bank below.

A	• —	H	• • • •	O	— — —	V	• • • —
B	— • • •	I	• •	P	• — — •	W	• — —
C	— • — •	J	• — — —	Q	— — • —	X	— • • —
D	— • •	K	— • —	R	• — •	Y	— • — —
E	•	L	• — • •	S	• • •	Z	— — • •
F	• • — •	M	— —	T	—		
G	— — •	N	— •	U	• • —		

First, write your message.

Then, look up the code for each letter and write it.

Use slash marks to separate the code for each letter.

Don't use periods—they'd be too confusing.

 **Helpful Hints**

wishes   I'm   codes'   hobbies   we'll
children   switches   ourselves   teacher's   can't

Plurals, possessives, contractions, syllables: Writing

UNIT 5 CHECKUP

Read each sentence. Fill in the circle next to the word that correctly completes the sentence. Write the word on the line.

1. Giant _____ are members of the deer family.
   ○ mooses
   ○ moose

2. There _____ ever been a larger animal with antlers.
   ○ has'nt
   ○ hasn't

3. Big as they are, moose can move as quietly as _____.
   ○ mice
   ○ mouses

4. Moose don't have many _____.
   ○ enemies
   ○ enemys

5. _____ are the animals they fear most.
   ○ Wolfs
   ○ Wolves

6. A moose has no front _____ in its upper jaw.
   ○ teeth
   ○ tooths

7. That means it _____ bite chunks of food.
   ○ cann't
   ○ can't

8. Water _____ soft leaves are a moose's favorite food.
   ○ plants'
   ○ plants's

9. Moose also pull leaves off tree _____.
   ○ branchs
   ○ branches

10. A moose can reach leaves growing twelve _____ above the ground!
    ○ feet
    ○ foots

11. Sometimes moose have twin _____.
    ○ calves
    ○ calfs

12. Moose _____ legs are very long.
    ○ calve's
    ○ calves'

13. A _____ new antlers grow in May.
    ○ moose's
    ○ mooses'

14. A bull moose's _____ can weigh 85 pounds!
    ○ antlers
    ○ antlers'

Tigers' Tongues and Dogs' Teeth

Paper money and coins haven't always been used as money. Stone Age people used the heads of axes for currency. The ancient Chinese used pieces of bronze cast in the shapes of things like shirts, knives, and hoes. You couldn't wear a tiny bronze shirt, but you could use it to buy a real shirt or a shirt's worth of anything else! Soldiers in Roman armies were paid in salt. In 1642, Virginia's General Assembly passed a law making tobacco the colony's only currency!

Around the world there have been many strange currencies: dogs' teeth in New Guinea, whales' teeth in the Pacific Islands, spearheads in Africa, and drums in Burma. In Thailand, tigers' tongues, claws, and teeth were used as money. Until about a hundred years ago, Asian banks issued blocks of tea as money. To make change, you'd break off pieces of the block! For many centuries, cowrie shells were accepted as money throughout much of Africa and Asia. In the French Sudan, people paid their taxes with cowries until 1907!

You can read the numbers on paper money, but long ago many people couldn't read. To help shepherds who didn't know how to read, one Welsh bank issued bank notes with pictures of sheep on them. The more sheep shown on a note, the more the note was worth!

1. What is the main idea of this passage?

_____

2. What could a tiny bronze knife buy in ancient China?

_____

3. What kind of money was used in Thailand?

_____

4. How did Welsh shepherds who couldn't read tell how much a bank note was worth? _____

What do you think the prefixes **bi** and **tri** mean? How are they alike?

Critical Thinking

Find the following items in the picture: a conductor, a triangle, a biplane, a tripod, a submarine, a bicycle, a superhero, a tricycle, a tractor, binoculars, triplets, and a propeller.

Home Letter

Dear Family,

As we work through this unit, we will be studying roots and prefixes—word parts that are added to the beginning of base words and roots to form new words.

At-Home Activities

▶ Ask your child to show you the pictures on the other side of this letter. (conductor, triangle, biplane, tripod, submarine, bicycle, superhero, tricycle, tractor, binoculars, triplets, propeller) Identify the prefixes and roots in the names of the items. (super-, bi-, tri-, sub-, con-, pro-, pel, duct, tract)

▶ With your child, look in magazines, newspapers, or homework papers for other words with prefixes and roots. Make a list of the words you find.

▶ Encourage your child to draw a picture with objects in it that begin with different prefixes and have you identify them.

Book Corner

You and your child might enjoy reading these books together. Look for them in your local library.

Doctor Coyote— A Native American Aesop's Fables

by John Bierhorst

Brilliantly retold fables and soft watercolor illustrations make a collection of entertaining and thought–provoking tales.

Jennifer-the-Jerk Is Missing

by Carol Gorman

A nerdy brat and his babysitter form an unlikely team in a suspenseful pursuit of kidnappers.

Sincerely,

_____

► **Read each word and circle the prefix un, dis, or non.**

1. nonpartisan
2. unclear
3. unkind
4. nonstop
5. undress
6. nonsense
7. nonessential
8. unfold
9. nonrestrictive
10. dislike
11. discover
12. unopened
13. disappear
14. unfamiliar
15. disinterested
16. nonfiction
17. nonproductive
18. unpleasant
19. disclose
20. nonexistent

► **Read each sentence. Complete the sentence by adding a prefix to the base word in parentheses.**

21. These books are _____ to me. (familiar)

22. I'd like to _____ what they're about. (cover)

23. I like reading _____ books. (fiction)

24. I can read a book _____ if it's good. (stop)

25. I don't _____ reading any kind of book. (like)

26. Reading is never _____ for me. (pleasant)

Read each word and circle its prefix.

1. irremovable   2. illiterate   3. irresponsible

4. irrational   5. illogical   6. irresistible

7. irrelevant   8. illegible   9. irreversible

Read the sentences below. Use the information in each sentence to help you write the meaning of the word in boldface print.

10. An argument that is logical makes sense. What is an **illogical** argument?

_____

_____

11. Something that is relevant has to do with the subject being discussed. What is something that is **irrelevant?** _____

_____

12. If a person's writing is legible, it is easy to read. What is **illegible** writing?

_____

_____

13. A person who is literate is able to read and write. What is an **illiterate** person? _____

_____

14. A person who is responsible can be depended upon and shows a strong sense of duty. What is an **irresponsible** person? _____

_____

15. Something that is removable is able to be removed. What is something that is **irremovable**? _____

_____

Read each word and circle its prefix.

The prefixes **im** and **in** can also mean **not**. The prefixes **em** and **en** mean **cause to be** or **to make**.

improper = not proper

incurable = not curable

empower = to make powerful

entangle = to make tangled

1. inflexible
2. entitled
3. enlarge
4. ineffective
5. impatient
6. impossible
7. embitter
8. inaccurately
9. encode
10. endanger
11. encase
12. imperfect

Rewrite each sentence below. Use one of the words from above to replace the underlined words.

13. The agent will <u>put</u> the secret message <u>in code</u>.

_____

_____

_____

14. Then the message will <u>not</u> be <u>possible</u> for just anyone to read.

_____

_____

_____

15. We don't want to <u>not accurately</u> encode the message.

_____

_____

_____

16. That might <u>put</u> someone in <u>danger</u>.

_____

_____

Uncovered Treasures of a Boy King

For centuries, people searched for undiscovered burial places of Egypt's pharaohs. Few had been left undisturbed. Yet incredibly, one tomb in the Royal Valley went untouched. This was the now-famous tomb of King Tutankhamen, discovered in 1922. King Tut, as he is often called, was an unimportant and almost unknown ruler who died in 1352 B.C. at the age of 19. Yet because Tut's tomb was found nearly intact, unlike most others, it remains the world's most exciting archaeological discovery.

No one encouraged British archaeologist Howard Carter in his search for King Tut's tomb. Most people felt that finding the tomb was impossible. They thought that Carter's insistence was irrational nonsense. Yet Carter would not be discouraged. After six years of digging, he finally unearthed the door of the tomb. He was not disappointed by the discoveries he made. Entombed with the young king were incredible treasures.

Perhaps the greatest treasure of all was the king's embalmed mummy, which was enclosed in a series of cases. The final one was solid gold! When the coffins were unsealed, Carter said, "The very air you breathe, unchanged through the centuries, you share with those who laid the mummy to its rest."

1. Why did people try to discourage Carter from searching for the tomb? _____

2. What word tells you that Carter was delighted by what he saw? _____

3. What does *unearthed* mean?

_____

4. What did Carter do when he unsealed the coffins?

_____

Why was the discovery of King Tutankhamen's tomb so special?

Critical Thinking

Name

Read each clue. Find the word in the word bank that matches the clue and write it on the lines. Then write the letters in order from 1–11 in the spaces below to answer the riddle.

RULE

Ex is a prefix that usually means **out from** or **beyond**. **Re** is a prefix that usually means **again** or **back**. **De** is a prefix that usually means **down from**, **away from**, or **the opposite**.

export = to send goods from one country to another

repay = to pay again or to pay back

depress = to press down

expense	defend	recount
destroy	repay	reunite
excavate	dethrone	rebound
	expand	

1. pay again or pay back   __ __ __ __ __ __
                                                    6

2. put off a throne   __ __ __ __ __ __ __ __
                                                        10

3. spring back   __ __ __ __ __ __ __
                              7   3

4. hollow out   __ __ __ __ __ __ __ __
                                  1

5. count again   __ __ __ __ __ __ __
                                            5

6. tear down; ruin   __ __ __ __ __ __ __
                                              11

7. cost; charge   __ __ __ __ __ __ __
                                  9

8. keep safe; protect   __ __ __ __ __ __
                              2

9. bring together again   __ __ __ __ __ __ __
                              8

10. grow larger   __ __ __ __ __ __
                              4

Riddle

What do you call a rabbit that tells jokes?

__ __ __ __ __ __ __ __ __ __ __

1. Tell why you might <u>return</u> something to a store.

_____

_____

2. Write about a time you wanted to <u>exchange</u> something with a friend.

_____

_____

3. Tell what you would do to <u>decode</u> a message.

_____

_____

4. Explain how a cook might <u>defrost</u> some frozen meat.

_____

_____

5. Tell why someone might <u>rewash</u> a bicycle.

_____

_____

6. Write a short news spot telling how the police <u>recaptured</u> a gorilla who escaped from the zoo.

_____

_____

7. List three things that can <u>explode</u>.

_____

_____

8. Tell two reasons why drivers might have to take a <u>detour</u> instead of their normal route.

_____

_____

Name _____

RULE

Co, com, and **con** are prefixes that can mean **with** or **together.**

cooperate = to work with others

compress = to press together

converse = to talk with others

1

compose   combat

2

conductor   convict

3

compete   combine

4

conversation   conclude

5

cosign   copilot

6

contest   connect

► Circle the prefix in each word. Then write a short definition of the word.

7. coauthor _____

8. conjoin _____

9. compact _____

10. coexist _____

11. compile _____

12. copilot _____

What is your opinion of the plans the scout troop made? Give reasons for your answer.

Critical Thinking

1. Jackie's scout troop is having a _____ to clean up the local parks.

contest
detest

2. The girls are trying to get everyone in their _____ involved.

community
compare

3. On Saturday, Jackie's troop held a meeting to _____ the rules.

explain
explode

4. They formed _____ to work together.

comments
committees

5. Jackie _____ the steps involved in cleaning up a park.

described
deported

6. Everyone at the meeting agreed to _____ in cleaning up the parks.

coauthor
cooperate

7. They _____ ideas about what they might do.

exchanged
exceeded

8. They would _____ debris from the hiking trails.

remove
resolve

9. They all hoped the city would _____ some of the broken picnic tables.

replace
refill

10. Before everyone _____, they wished each other luck.

designed
departed

Name _____

RULES

Read each word and circle its prefix.

The prefixes **fore, pre,** and **pro** have slightly different meanings.
forewarn = to warn before something happens
preheat = to heat ahead of time
project = to throw forward

1. forearm
2. prefix
3. preview
4. propel

5. pronoun
6. forenoon
7. prepare
8. forehead

9. produce
10. forefathers
11. foresight
12. prepay

Read each sentence. Fill in the circle beside the word that best completes the sentence. Write the word on the line.

13. Maria has _____ that she will be a great tennis player.
   ○ prorated   ○ prepaid   ○ proclaimed

14. Every day she practices her _____ and backhand shots.
   ○ forefather   ○ forehand   ○ project

15. She is working hard to _____ for a big tournament.
   ○ propel   ○ prepare   ○ foresee

16. Today she must play a _____ match to qualify for the tournament.
   ○ preliminary   ○ prefix   ○ prevention

17. Maria's coach _____ her that the competition would be stiff.
   ○ produced   ○ forewarned   ○ pretended

18. However, her coach _____ that she will make the tournament.
   ○ predicts   ○ prevents   ○ preserves

Read each clue. Find the word in the word bank that matches the clue. Then write the word in the crossword puzzle. There are more words in the list than you need.

forecast	forewarned	protect	promote	professional
pretend	presented	prepay	produce	forearm
preserve	forefathers	propose	protest	prepare

Across

2. to guard against harm or danger

3. to prepare food for later use by canning, pickling, or salting

5. to make an offer of marriage

7. a person who works in an occupation that requires special education and training

9. to raise to a higher rank or grade

10. to make believe as in a play

11. to give money ahead of time

Down

1. to tell or try to tell how something will turn out

3. to make something ready before the time that it is needed

4. to get ready for trouble before it comes

6. to speak out against, to object

7. shown

8. advised in advance

Lesson 69
Prefixes fore-, pre-, pro-

Name _____

Read each word and circle its prefix.

1. supervisor

2. overtime

3. overjoyed

4. oversleep

5. overcooked

6. supermarket

7. overcoat

8. superwoman

9. supervised

Read each sentence. Complete the sentence with a word from the list above.

10. Pat set her alarm clock so she wouldn't _____.

11. She was a _____, so she had to get to work before her employees.

12. Before work, Pat _____ her toast and burned it to a crisp.

13. It was raining so Pat put on her _____ and left for work.

14. Pat would have had to be a _____ to get all her work done.

15. There was so much work that Pat asked her staff to work

_____.

16. She _____ their work carefully.

17. On her way home, Pat stopped at the _____ to pick up some food.

18. Pat was _____ when she finally got home after her hard day.

Steve and Kim live outside the city in a suburban development. A vacant lot has been subdivided into small garden plots. The subsoil is rocky, but the topsoil is good for growing vegetables.

One morning Steve and Kim gathered outside, with all the other gardeners, underneath the sunny sky. Everyone worked together to cut away all the underbrush and clear away the rocks. Soon the vacant lot had undergone an outstanding change.

"It'll be great to have fresh lettuce and tomatoes for submarine sandwiches," said Kim.

There was an outburst of laughter as everyone agreed with Kim.

1. Where do Kim and Steve live? _____

_____

2. What part of the ground is rocky? _____

_____

3. What is underbrush? _____

_____

4. Why did everyone laugh when Kim mentioned lettuce and

tomatoes? _____

_____

How can you tell that Steve and Kim's neighbors all like one another?

Critical Thinking

Name _____

Twelve words containing the prefixes **bi-** and **tri-** are hidden in the puzzle. Some of the words go across, and some go down. Circle each word and write it next to its definition.

```
o  b  i  m  o  n  t  h  l  y
b  i  p  o  l  a  r  i  t  c
i  c  u  t  t  r  i  p  o  d
w  y  t  r  i  d  e  n  t  t
e  c  b  i  v  w  n  t  l  r
e  l  m  a  n  x  n  y  b  i
k  e  r  d  k  n  i  j  i  p
l  p  f  e  l  r  a  s  p  l
y  q  b  i  v  a  l  v  e  e
t  r  i  c  y  c  l  e  d  t
```

1. _____ happening every two weeks

2. _____ group of three

3. _____ vehicle with three wheels

4. _____ animal with two feet

5. _____ happening every three years

6. _____ having two poles

7. _____ happening every two months

8. _____ item having three legs

9. _____ vehicle with two wheels

10. _____ spear with three prongs

11. _____ one of three children born at the same time of the same mother

12. _____ shellfish with two shells

Read each word in the word bank and circle the prefixes semi and mid. Then read each definition and write the word from the word bank that goes with it.

semicircle

midsummer   midair   midway

semitropical   semifinal   midwinter

midwest   midterm   midshipman

1. the time of the year when January comes

2. a round or match that comes before the final one in a contest or tournament

3. the middle of a school semester

4. half of a circle

5. in the middle

6. near the tropical zone

Words beginning with the prefixes semi and mid are hidden in the puzzle below. Words go across and down. Circle each word in the puzzle. Then write it under the correct heading.

mid

_____

_____

_____

_____

semi

_____

_____

_____

```
A C E G M I M I D S U M M E R
M O Q S I U W Y A E D F H J L
N P M I D S H I P M A N R T V
X Z A C A Y Z B Q I D W E A T
D F H J I L N P R C T V X Z B
C E T G R M I D W I N T E R L
I K E M Y O G S U R W X Z A C
S E M I T R O P I C A L C E G
F S E M I F I N A L U W Y A I
K M F N P M I R T E Y M R T Y
```

> **Read the following words. Circle each word that contains the root pos. Underline each word that contains the root pel.**

> **DEFINITION**
>
> A **root** is a word part to which a prefix or suffix may be added to change its meaning. **Pos** usually means **put** or **place**. **Pel** usually means **push** or **drive**.
>
> **pos**ition = the way in which a person or thing is placed or arranged
>
> pro**pel** = to push or drive forward

1. posed
2. expel
3. impose
4. dispose
5. compose
6. repellent
7. compel
8. dispel
9. repose
10. expose

> **Read each sentence. Circle the meaning of the underlined word.**

11. Nan's mom <u>expelled</u> Nan's cat from the kitchen for jumping on the table.

    a. forcibly removed   b. politely excused

12. She <u>proposed</u> that the cat be banned from the kitchen at mealtimes.

    a. suggested   b. invited

13. Nan agreed and promised that the cat would not <u>impose</u> on her again.

    a. help   b. bother

14. With the cat problem <u>dispelled</u>, Nan could get back to her homework.

    a. surrounded   b. made to disappear

15. The only one <u>opposed</u> to the new rule was the cat.

    a. to be against   b. to be polite

1. import
2. rejection
3. projectile
4. eject
5. porter
6. report
7. injection
8. project
9. transportation

> **HINT**
>
> Here are some roots, or word parts, that appear in many English words. **Port** means **carry. Ject** means **throw** or **force.**
>
> **port**able = able to be carried
>
> e**ject** = to force out

▶ **Read each sentence. Circle the word that best completes the sentence and write the word on the line.**

10. A moving belt _____ materials along the assembly line.

| transported |
| projector |

11. Each worker added new parts to the _____ in front of him or her.

| portable |
| object |

12. Each step in the assembly procedure was _____.

| imported |
| important |

13. A poorly assembled machine would be _____ by the supervisor.

| rejected |
| projected |

14. The supervisor would make note of problems in an official _____.

| report |
| support |

15. No worker wanted to become the _____ of a supervisor's notes!

| inject |
| subject |

Name

1. Sam needed to finish his homework but was distracted by loud music.

_____

_____

2. He found his brother in the garage conducting his rock-and-roll band.

_____

3. The band had signed a contract to play at a school dance on Saturday.

_____

4. Sam asked if they could reduce the noise level so he could study.

_____

Read the words and the definitions. Write the number of each word on the line beside its definition.

5. deduct _____ to bring into view

6. conductor _____ to take or pull back

7. produce _____ to present one person to another

8. tractor _____ to subtract or take away from

9. retract _____ person who leads

10. introduce _____ to pull toward

11. attract _____ machine used for pulling

Look at each picture. Circle the word that describes the picture.

1

spectator   spectacular

2

subscribe   scribble

3

inspector   prospector

4

describe   subscription

5

respects   inspects

6

prescription   description

Read the words and the definitions. Write the number of each word on the line beside its definition.

7. inspector _____ one who watches rather than takes part in an event

8. description _____ something written, as on a coin or in a book

9. spectator _____ one who looks for profit

10. prescription _____ one who looks for clues or evidence

11. inscription _____ something written by a doctor

12. speculator _____ a detailed account

Name _____

Read each word. Write the number of vowels you see in each word. Then write the number of vowel sounds you hear.

	Vowels				**Vowels**	
	See	**Hear**			**See**	**Hear**
1. discomfort	_____	_____	**18.** inscription	_____	_____
2. supermarket	_____	_____	**19.** pronoun	_____	_____
3. demerit	_____	_____	**20.** enclose	_____	_____
4. triangle	_____	_____	**21.** bicycle	_____	_____
5. overseas	_____	_____	**22.** forenoon	_____	_____
6. nonresident	_____	_____	**23.** disappear	_____	_____
7. outcast	_____	_____	**24.** midnight	_____	_____
8. explode	_____	_____	**25.** recover	_____	_____
9. uncertain	_____	_____	**26.** contestant	_____	_____
10. preview	_____	_____	**27.** illegal	_____	_____
11. retract	_____	_____	**28.** objection	_____	_____
12. inspection	_____	_____	**29.** embitter	_____	_____
13. underweight	_____	_____	**30.** depress	_____	_____
14. combine	_____	_____	**31.** unhealthy	_____	_____
15. irregular	_____	_____	**32.** portable	_____	_____
16. repellent	_____	_____	**33.** coexist	_____	_____
17. semicircle	_____	_____	**34.** submarine	_____	_____

bi - plane

1. reject _____

2. irritate _____

3. conduct _____

4. employ _____

5. nonfiction _____

6. import _____

7. produce _____

8. induce _____

9. prescribe _____

10. unclean _____

11. compose _____

12. retract _____

13. illegal _____

14. repel _____

15. decription _____

16. underground _____

17. induct _____

18. important _____

19. report _____

20. distract _____

21. compel _____

22. enclose _____

23. expect _____

24. irregular _____

25. subject _____

26. inject _____

27. inspect _____

28. deduce _____

29. propel _____

30. nonsense _____

31. superhero _____

32. inscribe _____

33. detract _____

34. midday _____

35. illegible _____

36. bisect _____

Name _____

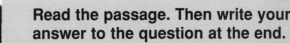

UNDERWATER EXPLORATION

The idea of underwater exploration has always attracted people. Impossible as it sounds, divers as long ago as the fourth century B.C. used breathing tubes to enable them to remain underwater for extended periods. Aristotle (384–322 B.C.) described a diving bell that consisted of a kettle held overhead. When submerged, the kettle remained filled with air. Illustrations in old manuscripts show divers wearing leather hoods with tubes near their foreheads that projected above the water—the first diving suits.

Beginning in the 1800s, diving suits encased wearers in rubber and metal to protect them from the cold and provide them with air. These uncomfortable, unsafe suits were connected to ships by long hoses through which air was propelled. Later, a tank worn on a diver's back was invented. This enabled a diver to swim without restriction. Recent improvements in diving gear enable divers to enjoy the incredible beauty of the underwater world in comfort.

Today, scientists explore the ocean depths in special submarines called submersibles. These can transport up to four people, who inspect the ocean through windows in the hull. Submersibles can hover midway between the surface and the bottom of the ocean.

Which invention in the article do you think is the most important for undersea exploration? Explain why.

_____
_____
_____
_____
_____
_____

Writing

Write a story about an underwater trip. Describe how you would go, with a scuba tank or in a submersible. What do you think you would see? The words in the word bank may help you.

Think of a good title for your story.

Who are the main characters?

What happens to them?

Use active verbs to make your writing interesting.

Include details.

Helpful Hints

unexpected	midway	conclude
depart	unforeseen	nonstop
impatiently	reassure	binoculars
	outline	

Name _____

Read each sentence. Fill in the circle next to the word that correctly completes the sentence. Write the word on the line.

1. **Two wheels** are to bicycle as **three wheels** are to _____.
   ○ triangle   ○ tricycle

2. **Possible** is to **impossible** as **sense** is to _____.
   ○ nonsense   ○ nonpayment

3. **Write** is to **story** as _____ is to **music.**
   ○ compose   ○ dispose

4. **Discover** is to **find** as _____ is to **happy.**
   ○ unhappy   ○ overjoyed

5. **Midsummer** is to **midwinter** as **midnight** is to _____.
   ○ midweek   ○ midday

6. **Inhale** is to **exhale** as **arrive** is to _____.
   ○ depart   ○ destroy

7. **Encourage** is to **discourage** as _____ is to **export.**
   ○ report   ○ import

8. **Coauthor** is to **book** as _____ is to **plane.**
   ○ copilot   ○ cosign

9. **Increase** is to **decrease** as **add** is to _____.
   ○ retract   ○ subtract

10. **Buried** is to **underground** as **submerged** is to _____.
   ○ overhead   ○ underwater

11. **Prospector** is to **mine** as _____ is to **train.**
   ○ conductor   ○ projector

12. **Biplane** is to **air** as _____ is to **water.**
   ○ submarine   ○ semicircle

▶ **Read the passage and answer the questions.**

Reduce, Reuse, Recycle

Our planet's natural resources can never be replaced. Although many of the world's environmental problems may seem overwhelming and impossible to combat, we can prevent further destruction. Here are a few ideas to enable you to conduct a war on waste.

Reduce Many things come packaged in unnecessary layers. When we unwrap and remove a purchase, we discard the packaging. Plastic packaging is produced from oil extracted from underground wells. That oil can never be reused or replaced. Discarded as trash, plastic takes centuries to decompose. What can you do?
   ▶ Refuse to purchase products that employ excessive packaging.

Reuse People have always reused things to create new ones. Stone Age people didn't discard broken stone tools. They reshaped them into new tools. What can you do?
   ▶ Buy eggs in cardboard cartons. Reuse the cartons for art projects.

Recycle Glass, metal, paper, and some kinds of plastic can be recycled. Many communities encourage or even require residents to recycle these reusable materials. What can you do?
   ▶ Collect recyclable materials and take them to your local recycling center.

1. What three words are the keys to helping save the earth?

_____

2. What is the problem with many things we purchase?

_____

3. How can people reduce waste?

_____

4. What kinds of materials can be recycled?

_____

_____

Have You Ever Seen?

Have you ever seen a sheet on a river bed?
Or a single hair from a hammer's head?
Has the foot of a mountain any toes?
And is there a pair of garden hose?

Does a needle ever wink its eye?
Why doesn't the wing of a building fly?
Can you write notes with a pen full of sheep?
Or open the trunk of a tree for a peep?

Are the teeth of a saw ever going to bite?
Have the hands of a clock any left or right?
Can the garden plot be deep and dark?
And what is the sound of a birch tree's bark?

—Anonymous

In the poem, the words bed, foot, eye, wing, pen, and trunk have more than one meaning. Tell how each word is used in the poem and then give a second meaning for each word.

Critical Thinking

Home Letter

Dear Family,

Over the next few weeks, your child will learn about synonyms, antonyms, and homonyms. We will also be practicing dictionary skills.

At-Home Activities

▶ Read the poem "Have You Ever Seen?" on the other side of this letter with your child. Talk about the two meanings of bed and how the double meaning makes the line funny. Then look through the poem for other words with more than one meaning.

▶ Think of homonyms for pair (pear, pare) and eye (I). Ask your child to find the antonyms left and right in the last verse.

▶ Encourage your child to pick out three words in the poem with double meanings and draw a picture to illustrate each meaning.

Book Corner

You and your child might enjoy reading these books together. Look for them in your local library.

Flights of Fancy and Other Poems

by Myra Cohn Livingston

Forty poems that challenge children's perceptions of the world by adding poetic dimensions to everyday surroundings are to be enjoyed in this unique collection.

The Celery Stalks at Midnight

by James Howe

Fans of Chester the cat, Howard the dog, and the ever-evasive "vegetable vampire" Bunnicula will love the fun and puns of this adventure.

Sincerely,

_____

Name _____

Circle the words in the puzzle that are synonyms for the numbered words. Write the words you find.

```
n  e  a  t  b  q  p
g  h  a  r  m  u  r
r  c  g  i  j  i  h
i  n  s  p  e  c  t
n  a  q  u  z  k  o
```

1. journey _____

2. tidy _____

3. rapid _____

4. hurt _____

5. examine _____

6. smile _____

Read the passage. Write a synonym from the word bank below for each word in parentheses to complete each sentence.

| strength | providing | simply | saying | quantity | varying |
| speech | create | whole | used | ideas | speed |

Without _____ a word, the Mazateco people of Mexico can carry on
1. (speaking)

_____ conversations. They do this _____ by whistling!
2. (entire)   3. (just)

This unusual form of _____ is _____ only by the men
4. (language)   5. (employed)

of the tribe. They get across _____ by _____ the
6. (thoughts)   7. (changing)

_____, pitch, and _____ of the whistles. Traders
8. (quickness)   9. (force)

can _____ deals by _____ exact details of
10. (make)   11. (giving)

_____ and price without saying a word!
12. (amount)

Read the first word in each row. Then circle the words in the row that are synonyms for the first word.

1	**walk**	stroll	saunter	trudge	tumble	march
2	**cold**	chilly	creep	cool	icy	freezing
3	**hot**	warm	heated	joyful	boiling	roasting
4	**quick**	swift	fast	rapid	gloomy	speedy
5	**strong**	powerful	lengthy	hardy	vigorous	forceful
6	**weak**	happy	frail	feeble	fragile	sickly

Unscramble the letters in the word bank to find a synonym for each word. Write the word on the line. The first letter will help you.

heir   simot   dubot   varbe   recof   pealse

7. damp   m___ ___ ___ ___

8. compel   f___ ___ ___ ___

9. mistrust   d___ ___ ___ ___

10. courageous   b___ ___ ___ ___

11. employ   h___ ___ ___

12. satisfy   p___ ___ ___ ___ ___

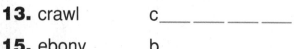

perec   pdira   raleg   pphay   akblc   alsml

13. crawl   c___ ___ ___ ___

14. little   s___ ___ ___ ___

15. ebony   b___ ___ ___ ___

16. content   h___ ___ ___ ___

17. swift   r___ ___ ___ ___

18. huge   l___ ___ ___ ___

Name _____

▶ **Read the first word in each row. Then circle the words in the row that are antonyms of the first word.**

DEFINITION

Antonyms are words that are opposite or almost opposite in meaning.

happy—sad   large—small

1	**slow**	quick	happy	fast	rapid	swift
2	**sweet**	sour	tart	bitter	sugary	unsweet
3	**weak**	strong	hardy	powerless	powerful	forceful
4	**safe**	secure	uncertain	insecure	unsafe	unprotected
5	**forbid**	allow	refuse	permit	tolerate	approve
6	**distrust**	trust	faith	belief	disbelief	confidence

▶ **Read each pair of sentences. Find the word in the first sentence that is an antonym of a word in the second sentence. Underline the two words.**

7. Leah had just started skating and found it difficult.

8. Ted had been skating for years and made it look easy.

9. Ted felt that Leah was getting much better at skating.

10. Every time Leah fell, she felt she was just getting worse.

11. It was early when they started skating.

12. Leah and Ted skated until late in the day.

13. Around four o'clock Ted and Leah became tired.

14. Then they went home to get rested.

Find the antonym in the word bank for each of the following words. Write each antonym on the line beside the word.

| tasty | quiet | joyful | follow | narrow | frown | hard | fresh |

1. soft ___ ___ ___ ___

2. bland ___ ___ ___ ___ ___

3. noisy ___ ___ ___ ___ ___

4. wide ___ ___ ___ ___ ___

5. smile ___ ___ ___ ___ ___

6. unhappy ___ ___ ___ ___ ___

7. stale ___ ___ ___ ___ ___

8. lead ___ ___ ___ ___ ___

Read each sentence and the pair of words that follows. Choose the word that best completes the sentence and write the word on the line.

9. For the first time the usually honest boy was _____ about his behavior.

untruthful

truthful

10. He said he would take the fastest way home, but he took the _____.

quickest

slowest

11. His mother was unhappy with him but was _____ to see he was safe.

disappointed

overjoyed

12. The hungry boy devoured his food and was soon _____.

full

empty

13. Then he took off his dirty clothes and put on some _____ pajamas.

soiled

clean

14. Feeling tired, he went to bed so he would be _____ the next day.

rested

exhausted

Name _____

> **Read each pair of sentences. Find the word in the first sentence that sounds like a word in the second sentence. Write the two words on the lines.**

DEFINITION

Homonyms are words that sound alike but have different meanings and usually different spellings.

to—two—too   no—know

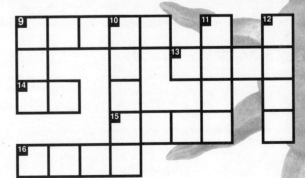

1. Road construction was a triumph of the Roman Empire.   _____

2. Travelers rode on 50,000 miles of Roman highways.   _____

3. A traveler from Rome could get to London in six days.   _____

4. The traveling time between the two cities was not improved for 1,500 years!   _____

5. Roman roads passed ancient monuments and temples.   _____

6. They brought travelers to great cities of the past.   _____

7. Roman roads went through Europe, the Middle East, and Africa.   _____

8. People threw up their hands in wonder at this achievement.   _____

> **Complete the puzzle. Write the homonym from the word bank for each clue word.**

| sun | hare | eight | pale | blew | no | steel | meat | sail |

Across

9. steal
13. sale
14. know
15. hair
16. meet

Down

9. son
10. ate
11. pail
12. blue

Circle the name of each picture.

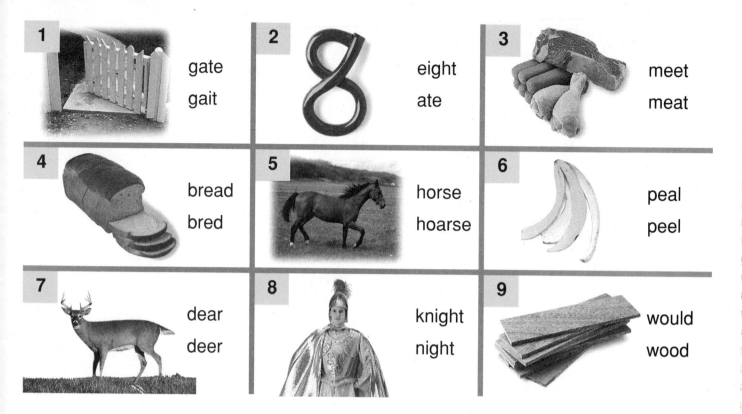

1 gate / gait

2 eight / ate

3 meet / meat

4 bread / bred

5 horse / hoarse

6 peal / peel

7 dear / deer

8 knight / night

9 would / wood

Read each sentence and the pair of words that follows. Choose the word that best completes the sentence and write the word on the line.

10. Our _____, Mrs. Fox, visited our class.

principle
principal

11. Our class read _____ for her.

aloud
allowed

12. Then we showed her how well we can _____.

right
write

13. Our math homework was _____ today.

due
dew

14. The problems were _____ very hard.

knot
not

15. We _____ Mrs. Fox was proud of us.

know
no

16. She told us _____ keep up the good work.

two
to

Name _____

▶ **Write the words in each group in alphabetical order.**

HINTS

Words in a dictionary are arranged in alphabetical order. When words begin with the same letter or letters, look at the second or third letter to put the words in alphabetical order.

j<u>a</u>y   ju<u>d</u>ge

j<u>e</u>an   ju<u>g</u>

j<u>o</u>g   jui<u>c</u>e

1. pearl   _____

    pin   _____

    powder   _____

    part   _____

    photo   _____

2. door   _____

    duty   _____

    date   _____

    drain   _____

    digest   _____

3. llama   _____

    lucky   _____

    lodge   _____

    lying   _____

    lizard   _____

▶ **Write the names of the animals in the word bank in alphabetical order. Use the dictionary to find out about the animals you do not know.**

panda	peacock
parrot	porpoise
rhinoceros	rabbit
raccoon	raven
toucan	tortoise
tiger	turtle

4. _____

5. _____

6. _____

7. _____

8. _____

9. _____

10. _____

11. _____

12. _____

13. _____

14. _____

15. _____

Lesson 80
Alphabetical order

175

Read each word and figure out in which section of the dictionary you would find this word. Use the picture in the box to help you. Then write the word first, second, third, or fourth on the line next to each word.

1. banquet _____

2. impostor _____

3. frontier _____

4. turret _____

5. privilege _____

6. repeal _____

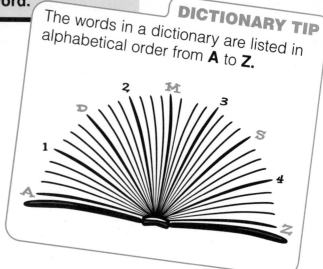

DICTIONARY TIP

The words in a dictionary are listed in alphabetical order from **A** to **Z**.

 See how quickly you can find these words in the dictionary. Then write each word on the line beside its definition.

petunia	visibility	barnacle	crest
jerkin	abacus	redwood	easel

7. used for doing math quickly without writing _____

8. a standing frame for holding an artist's painting _____

9. a short, tight jacket often without sleeves _____

10. a plant with flowers of various colors _____

11. a giant evergreen tree found in California and Oregon _____

12. a small sea animal with a shell which fastens itself to rocks and the bottom of boats _____

13. the distance within which things are visible _____

14. a tuft of feathers or fur on the head of some birds and animals _____

▶ **Look at each pair of guide words and the words below them. Cross out any words that would not be found on the same page as those guide words. Then write the remaining words in alphabetical order on the lines.**

1	**fluffy • fold**	**2**	**muddle • napkin**	**3**	**safety • sauce**
fly	_____	nap	_____	salad	_____
foil	_____	much	_____	satisfy	_____
foot	_____	mystery	_____	salt	_____
focus	_____	nation	_____	sad	_____

4	**oar • oft**	**5**	**penny • pizza**	**6**	**job • jug**
object	_____	plain	_____	jog	_____
office	_____	people	_____	jut	_____
occur	_____	piano	_____	jolt	_____
out	_____	perfect	_____	join	_____

▶ **Look at each pair of guide words. Circle the words that would be on the same page as the guide words. Then number the circled words in each column in alphabetical order.**

7	**ant • apple**	**8**	**dose • drake**	**9**	**machine • make**
____	apart	____	down	____	major
____	apt	____	doze	____	male
____	apologize	____	dot	____	magazine
____	any	____	dream	____	maid

osprey   rasp   moat   mirror   mixer   ornament

moist   ours   ought   rake   raft   ram

1. mineral • model

_____

_____

_____

2. organ • ounce

_____

_____

_____

3. radio • rank

_____

_____

_____

Read the information in each exercise. Decide whether the word would appear **before, on,** or **after** the dictionary page with those guide words. Write your answer on the line.

4. You open the dictionary and see the guide words **firm • fixture**.
Would the word **fist** come _before, on_ or _after_ this dictionary page? _____

5. You open the dictionary and see the guide words **grief • grotto**.
Would the word **grew** come _before, on_ or _after_ this dictionary page? _____

6. You open the dictionary and see the guide words **code • comic**.
Would the word **collar** come _before, on_ or _after_ this dictionary page? _____

7. You open the dictionary and see the guide words **swell • swine**.
Would the word **sword** come _before, on_ or _after_ this dictionary page? _____

Name _____

Many words that begin with **un, re,** or **dis** or end with **s, es, ing, ed, er,** or **est** are not listed as separate entry words in the dictionary. To find the meaning of these words, look up the base word to which the prefix or ending has been added. Abbreviations and contractions are listed alphabetically in the dictionary as though they were whole words.

DICTIONARY TIPS
The words shown in boldface print in the dictionary are called **entry words.** All the information about an entry word is called an **entry.**

Read each word. Then write the entry word you would look up in the dictionary. Remember that if a word has a common prefix or suffix, you may need to look up the base word to which the prefix or suffix has been added.

1. poodles _____

2. wider _____

3. clouds _____

4. racing _____

5. knitting _____

6. angriest _____

7. permitted _____

8. rewrap _____

9. corrected _____

10. darkness _____

11. ivies _____

12. omitting _____

13. rained _____

14. pennies _____

15. repack _____

16. dryly _____

For each group, number the abbreviations and contractions in alphabetical order. Then write the word or phrase each stands for.

17. ___ M.D. _____

___ lb _____

___ km _____

___ CA _____

___ Fri. _____

18. ___ can't _____

___ they'll _____

___ who's _____

___ here's _____

___ we've _____

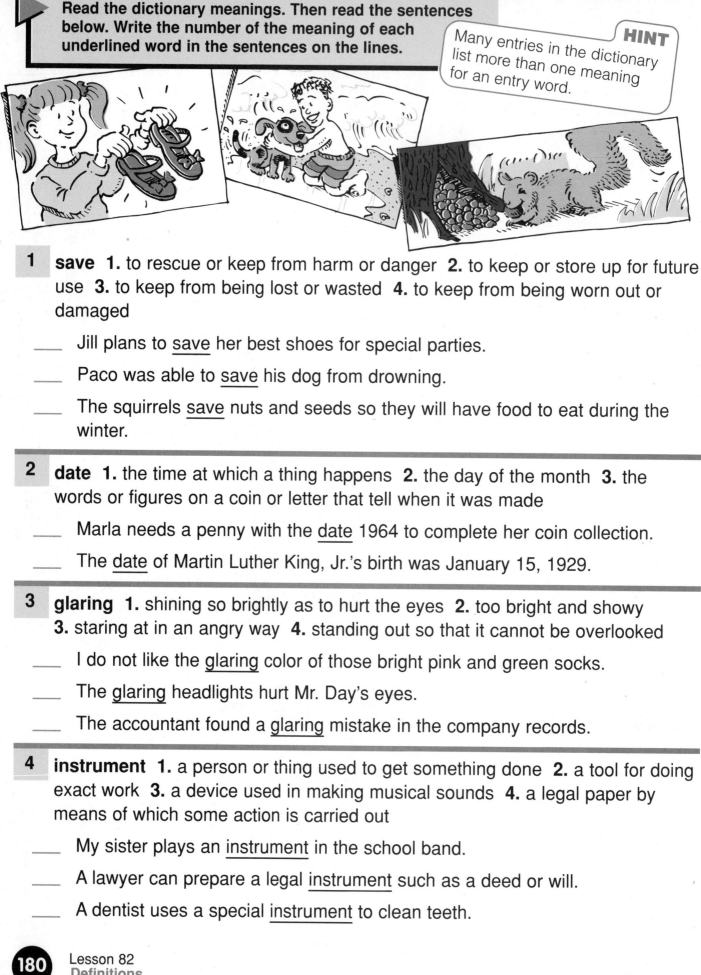

Read the dictionary meanings. Then read the sentences below. Write the number of the meaning of each underlined word in the sentences on the lines.

HINT
Many entries in the dictionary list more than one meaning for an entry word.

1 **save** **1.** to rescue or keep from harm or danger **2.** to keep or store up for future use **3.** to keep from being lost or wasted **4.** to keep from being worn out or damaged

____ Jill plans to <u>save</u> her best shoes for special parties.

____ Paco was able to <u>save</u> his dog from drowning.

____ The squirrels <u>save</u> nuts and seeds so they will have food to eat during the winter.

2 **date** **1.** the time at which a thing happens **2.** the day of the month **3.** the words or figures on a coin or letter that tell when it was made

____ Marla needs a penny with the <u>date</u> 1964 to complete her coin collection.

____ The <u>date</u> of Martin Luther King, Jr.'s birth was January 15, 1929.

3 **glaring** **1.** shining so brightly as to hurt the eyes **2.** too bright and showy **3.** staring at in an angry way **4.** standing out so that it cannot be overlooked

____ I do not like the <u>glaring</u> color of those bright pink and green socks.

____ The <u>glaring</u> headlights hurt Mr. Day's eyes.

____ The accountant found a <u>glaring</u> mistake in the company records.

4 **instrument** **1.** a person or thing used to get something done **2.** a tool for doing exact work **3.** a device used in making musical sounds **4.** a legal paper by means of which some action is carried out

____ My sister plays an <u>instrument</u> in the school band.

____ A lawyer can prepare a legal <u>instrument</u> such as a deed or will.

____ A dentist uses a special <u>instrument</u> to clean teeth.

Name _____

> **Read the dictionary entries. Then choose one of the words to complete each sentence below. Write the word and the correct definition number on the line.**

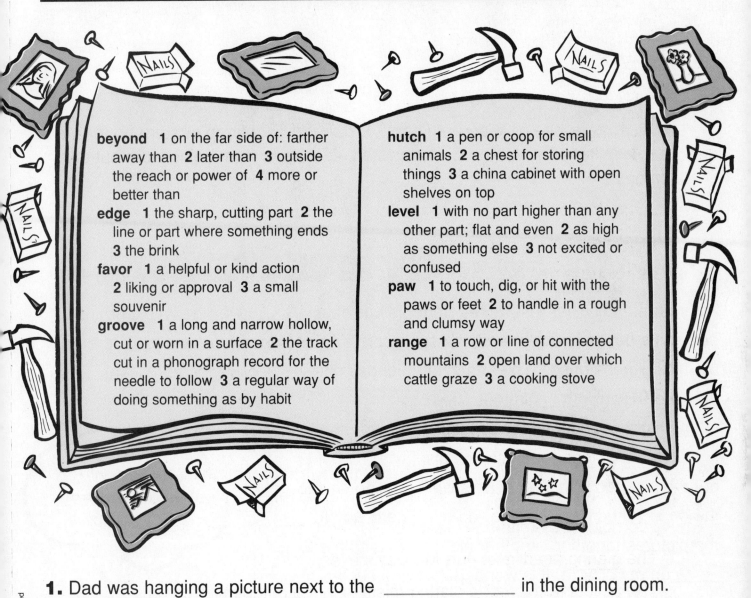

beyond 1 on the far side of: farther away than 2 later than 3 outside the reach or power of 4 more or better than

edge 1 the sharp, cutting part 2 the line or part where something ends 3 the brink

favor 1 a helpful or kind action 2 liking or approval 3 a small souvenir

groove 1 a long and narrow hollow, cut or worn in a surface 2 the track cut in a phonograph record for the needle to follow 3 a regular way of doing something as by habit

hutch 1 a pen or coop for small animals 2 a chest for storing things 3 a china cabinet with open shelves on top

level 1 with no part higher than any other part; flat and even 2 as high as something else 3 not excited or confused

paw 1 to touch, dig, or hit with the paws or feet 2 to handle in a rough and clumsy way

range 1 a row or line of connected mountains 2 open land over which cattle graze 3 a cooking stove

1. Dad was hanging a picture next to the _____ in the dining room.

2. He asked Dan to do him a _____ and get a hammer.

3. There was a hammer in the kitchen next to the _____.

4. Before Dad hung the picture, he asked Dan if it was _____.

5. Dan set the hammer on the _____ of the table, and it fell.

6. Dad tried to pick it up, but it was _____ his reach.

7. Dan was upset because the hammer made a _____ in the floor.

DEFINITION

Homographs are words that are spelled alike, but have different meanings. In the dictionary, entry words that are homographs have a small raised number to the right of the word.

clip¹ to cut off or cut out with scissors.
clip² to fasten things together
firm¹ that stays the same; not changing.
firm² a business company
kind¹ sort of variety.
kind² ready to help others.
pick¹ a heavy metal tool with a pointed end.

pick² to choose or select.
tire¹ to be unable to go on because of a need for rest.
tire² rubber tube filled with air on a wheel.

A Visit from My Grandfather

My grandfather has just retired from his business _____. Over the weekend, he
(1)
helped us get the garden ready for spring planting. He used a heavy _____ to break
(2)
up thick clumps of soil. Then each of us chose one _____ of vegetable to plant. This
(3)
hard work didn't _____ him out.
(4)

One night Grandfather and I looked through magazines to
find pictures of food for a science display. He would _____
(5)
out the pictures with long shears while my job was to _____
(6)
the ones I liked best. He showed me a neat way to _____
(7)
the pictures together. Another night he helped me fix a flat
_____ on my bicycle. It is wonderful having such a _____
(8)   (9)
grandfather, and I know he will always be a _____ friend.
(10)

How can you tell that the narrator loves his grandfather?

1. _____
2. _____
3. _____
4. _____
5. _____

6. _____
7. _____
8. _____
9. _____
10. _____

Critical Thinking

Name _____

The beginning sound in **choir** is **k** as in **keep**. Find **k** in the first column and look over to the next column to find words that have different spellings of the **k** sound. After you find the correct letter combinations for the beginning of a word, you should be able to find the word.

Every dictionary has a pronunciation key that shows various spellings for different sounds.

Pronunciation Key
consonant sounds

d	no**d**, ri**dd**le, call**ed**	l	**l**eave, ca**ll**, is**l**and
f	**f**ix, di**ff**erent, lau**gh**, **ph**one, cal**f**	m	dru**m**, dru**mm**er, li**mb**, hy**mn**, cal**m**
g	**g**ive, e**gg**, **gh**ost, **gu**ard	n	**n**ear, di**nn**er, **gn**ome, **kn**eel, **pn**eumonia
h	**h**er, **wh**o	n	lo**ng**, thi**nk**, to**ng**ue
j	**j**am, **g**em, exa**gg**erate, **g**raduate, sol**di**er, ju**dg**ment, a**dj**ust	p	ho**p**, di**pp**er
		r	**r**iver, be**rr**y, **rh**yme, **wr**ong
k	**k**ite, wal**k**, **c**an, a**cc**ount, **ch**rome, lu**ck**, la**cq**uer, bis**c**uit, li**qu**or	s	**s**it, mi**ss**, **sc**ience, **c**ent, **ps**ychology, **sch**ism

Use the pronunciation key above to help you circle the correct spelling, You may also need to check a dictionary.

1. Find a word that rhymes with **pail** and means "a small wild bird."

quail   kwail   chwail

2. Find a word that rhymes with **ham** and means "a baby sheep."

lam   lamb   lalm

3. Find a word that rhymes with **best** and means "a visitor."

gest   thest   guest

4. Find a word that rhymes with **bat** and means "a small flying insect."

gnat   nat   pant

5. Find a word that rhymes with **string** and means "to twist with force."

rhing   wring   ring

6. Find a word that rhymes with **went** and means "a smell, an odor."

cent   sent   scent

7. Find a word that rhymes with **craze** and means "disturb or upset."

phase   faze   fase

The **respelling** that follows a dictionary entry shows you how to pronounce the word. The dictionary **pronunciation key** can help you pronounce each sound shown in the respelling.

Pronunciation Key

Symbol	Key Words	Symbol	Key Words	Symbol	Key Words
b	**b**ed	m	**m**eat	y	**y**ard
d	**d**og	n	**n**ose	z	**z**ebra
f	**f**all	p	**p**ut	ch	**ch**in, ar**ch**
g	**g**et	r	**r**ed	ŋ	ri**ng**, dri**nk**
h	**h**elp	s	**s**ee, **c**ircle	sh	**sh**e, pu**sh**
j	**j**ump, **g**ym	t	**t**op	th	**th**in, tru**th**
k	**k**iss, **c**all	v	**v**at	*th*	**th**en, fa**th**er
l	**l**eg	w	**w**ish	zh	mea**s**ure

Study the consonant sounds above taken from a dictionary pronunciation key. Then read each riddle. Use the pronunciation key to help you say each respelling that answers the riddle. Then write each word from the word bank on the line beside its respelling.

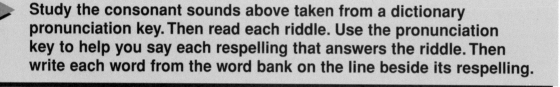

clock	glove	scales	comb	holes	crane
light	rose	fence	quick	lettuce	ice

1. What goes around a yard but doesn't move?

a fens _____

2. What can lie in a bed but can't sleep?

a rōz _____

3. What has two hands but no arms?

a klok _____

4. What bird can lift the most?

a krān _____

5. What can go through water without getting wet?

līt _____

6. What is the hardest thing about learning to skate?

the īs _____

7. What has teeth but no mouth?

a kōm _____

8. What has a head but no brain?

letis _____

Study the long and short vowel sounds from a dictionary pronunciation key. Pronounce each example word and listen for the vowel sound.

Pronunciation Key

Symbol	Key Words	Symbol	Key Words
a	cat	i	fit, here
ā	ape	ī	ice, fire
e	ten, berry	ō	go
ē	me	u	up

Read the respellings below. Each one contains a symbol from the key above. Beside each respelling, write the example words from the pronunciation key that show you how to pronounce the symbol. Write the entry word for each respelling.

1. (tīr) _____ _____

2. (grēt) _____ _____

3. (lāt) _____ _____

4. (mis) _____ _____

5. (stōv) _____ _____

6. (plāt) _____ _____

7. (pas) _____ _____

8. (fus) _____ _____

9. (bred) _____ _____

10. (mīs) _____ _____

11. (bluf) _____ _____

12. (krēm) _____ _____

13. (stik) _____ _____

14. (smel) _____ _____

Study more vowel sounds taken from a dictionary pronunciation key. Pronounce each example word and listen for the vowel sound.

HINT

In addition to long and short vowel sounds, the pronunciation key also contains other vowel sounds.

Pronunciation Key

Symbol	Key Words	Symbol	Key Words
ä	cot, car	ʉ	fur, shirt
ô	fall, for	ə	a in **ago**
oi	**oi**l		e in ag**e**nt
oo	l**oo**k, p**u**ll		i in penc**i**l
ōo	t**oo**l, r**u**le		o in at**o**m
ou	**ou**t, cr**ow**d		u in circ**u**s

 Use the pronunciation key to help you say each respelling. Then write each word from the word bank on the line beside its respelling.

liner	clause	purr	room
cart	pure	close	lose
cartoon	apart	heir	car
lot	round	use	purse
word	loss	line	hair

1. (klôz) _____

2. (kärt) _____

3. (kär) _____

4. (lät) _____

5. (rōom) _____

6. (lōoz) _____

7. (wʉrd) _____

8. (yōoz) _____

9. (pʉrs) _____

10. (pyoor) _____

11. (lôs) _____

12. (lin´ər) _____

13. (hār) _____

14. (ə pärt´) _____

Lesson 85
The pronunciation key

Name _____

▶ **For each word below, the respelling is shown. Place the accent mark where it belongs. You may check your dictionary, if necessary.**

HINT

In a word with two or more syllables, one syllable is **accented** or **stressed** more than the others. In the dictionary, an accent mark (´) is placed after the syllable that is said with more stress.

da´ līt (daylight)

den´ tist (dentist)

i las´ tik (elastic)

1. iceberg (īs burg)

2. event (ə vent)

3. deny (dē nī)

4. jacket (jack ət)

5. obey (ō bā)

6. office (ôf is)

7. relieve (rē lēv)

8. harvest (här vəst)

9. ruin (r͞oo in)

10. invite (in vīt)

▶ **Read each sentence. Circle the respelling of the underlined word that makes sense in the sentence.**

HINT

Sometimes a word can be pronounced in different ways depending on its meaning. In this case, the accent may shift to another syllable.

11. Olivia's favorite birthday <u>present</u> was a new bike.

prez´ ənt
pre zent´

12. She also liked the <u>record</u> of her favorite song.

re kôrd´
rek´ ərd

13. Her sister gave her a puzzle with a picture of a sandy <u>desert</u>.

də zurt´
dez´ ərt

14. Her big <u>project</u> now is to write thank you notes.

prä´ jekt
prə jekt´

Read the passage. Choose the word from the word bank that will complete each sentence. Write the word on the line. You will use each word twice.

"Just look at all the _____ 1 in the park!"

the ranger said. "Each _____ 2 was

carelessly thrown away by some litterbug. At

| present | refuse |
| record | object |

_____ 3 the park is dangerous and unhealthy.

Does anyone here _____ 4 to picking up trash?"

"No!" they said. "We won't _____ 5 to help."

"Great!" said the ranger. "Let's try to set a speed

_____ 6 for cleaning up the park. The town will

_____ 7 prizes to the volunteers who collect

the most trash. I'll _____ 8 the number of bags

each of you turns in."

Read the passage again. For each word you wrote, find and circle the correct respelling below.

9		**10**		**11**		**12**	
refuse	ref´ yooz	object	ob jekt´	present	prē zent´	object	ob jekt´
	ri fyooz´		ob´jekt		prez´ənt		ob´jekt

13		**14**		**15**		**16**	
refuse	ref´yooz	record	rek´ərd	present	prē zent´	record	rek´ərd
	ri fyooz´		ri kôrd´		prez´ənt		ri kôrd´

Name _____

Deserts: HOT or COLD?

What do you think of when you hear the word *desert*? Probably you picture a hot, sandy, dry place with no water, not even a drop of dew. That describes some deserts, but not all.

The definition of a desert is an area that receives less than ten inches of rainfall a year. That includes the hot, arid reaches of the North African Sahara, where daytime temperatures reach 120°F. It also includes the frigid, icy continent of Antarctica, where winter temperatures drop to -70°F! Even deserts that are roasting during the day can be cold at night. A temperature drop of more than 60° between midday and midnight is not uncommon.

A desert is not a deserted place. Where there is even a small amount of moisture, cactus and other desert plants can grow. When the quantity of water is greater, animals live and flourish, too. Many kinds of snakes, lizards, small mammals, birds, and insects reside in the sandy wastes of deserts.

Deserts are also home to people. In the Sonoran Desert of the American Southwest, there is enough moisture for water-storing plants, such as the saguaro cactus, to thrive. For the Papago people who live there, the fruit of the saguaro is an important food source. In Tibet, the world's highest desert, the ground might look bare, but the soil can bear enough plants to feed the goats, sheep, and yaks kept by herders.

If you were going to spend time in a desert, what five things would you take with you and why?

_____

_____

_____

_____

Writing

As a world traveler, you have visited one of the three types of desert mentioned. Write an E-mail letter to a friend describing what you saw there. Use words from the word bank.

_____

_____

_____

_____

_____

_____

_____

_____

_____

_____

_____

_____

_____

_____

_____

_____

_____

_____

Decide what mood you want your description to create.

Make a list of words to describe how the desert looked, sounded, smelled, and felt.

Describe how the desert made you feel.

Helpful Hints

arid	record	wasteland
wind	oasis	inhabitants
fiery	vast	moisture
	barren	

Lesson 87
Synonyms, antonyms, homonyms, dictionary skills: Writing

Read each sentence. Decide whether the two underlined words are synonyms, antonyms, or homonyms. Fill in the circle beside your choice.

1. Tina <u>read</u> a book called **The <u>Red</u> Shawl** for school.
○ synonyms   ○ antonyms   ○ homonyms

2. The story was about an <u>elderly</u> woman and her <u>young</u> granddaughter.
○ synonyms   ○ antonyms   ○ homonyms

3. They <u>would</u> often sit on the <u>wood</u> porch swing and talk.
○ synonyms   ○ antonyms   ○ homonyms

4. <u>Whether</u> the <u>weather</u> was cloudy or not, Grandma always wore a red shawl.
○ synonyms   ○ antonyms   ○ homonyms

5. Grandma told Tina <u>amazing</u> stories about her <u>wonderful</u> life.
○ synonyms   ○ antonyms   ○ homonyms

6. As a young woman, Grandma had gone to <u>sea</u> to <u>see</u> the world.
○ synonyms   ○ antonyms   ○ homonyms

7. She had bought the <u>lovely</u> red shawl in a <u>beautiful</u> seaside town.
○ synonyms   ○ antonyms   ○ homonyms

8. The red shawl helped her <u>remember</u> adventures she never wanted to <u>forget</u>.
○ synonyms   ○ antonyms   ○ homonyms

Read each sentence. Fill in the circle next to the respelling of the underlined word that makes sense in the sentence.

9. The explorer looked out over the vast sandy <u>desert</u>.
○ di zûrt´   ○ dez´ ərt

10. The searing hot <u>wind</u> scorched his face.
○ wind   ○ wīnd

11. His research <u>project</u> had taken him to many amazing places.
○ prä´ jekt   ○ prə jekt´

12. He had come <u>close</u> to danger many times.
○ kloz   ○ klōs

An Animal Oddity

When European scientists first saw the skin of an Australian platypus in 1797, they were convinced it was a hoax. They believed the skins of several different animals had been stitched together. It was no trick. The odd and amazing platypus really does look as if a number of animals have been sewn together to create this strange creature! Covered with thick fur as soft as a mole's, the platypus has the bill of a duck, webbed feet, and the tail of a beaver. Even more astonishing, this unusual mammal hatches from an egg!

At dawn and at dusk, the platypus emerges from its burrow near a stream to feed. Using its tail as a rudder, it swims close to the stream bottom. Employing its soft bill as a shovel, it probes in the mud for crayfish, worms, and other creatures to eat. To protect themselves, male platypuses are equipped with poisonous spurs on the ankles of their hind feet. Any animal chasing the small platypus through the water must avoid its poisonous kick. One scratch from a spur can kill a creature as large as a dog!

1. Which word in the passage is a synonym for *hoax*?

_____

2. Why did scientists think the platypus skin was a hoax?

_____

_____

3. Which two words in the passage are synonyms for *odd*?

_____

4. What meaning does the word *bill* have in this passage?

_____

5. Which word in the passage is an antonym for *dawn*?

_____

6. Find two antonyms in the last two sentences of the passage.

_____